Colene Ledford has produced a thought-provoking and controversial book that is sure to have readers reaching for their Bibles. This is must reading for anyone interested in End-Time prophecy and specifically who it is that makes up the Bride of Christ. Readers are challenged to live their lives in such a way that they are pleasing to our Lord and Savior, Jesus Christ.

—DR. DANIEL J. TYLER
PRESIDENT, INTERNATIONAL SEMINARY
PLYMOUTH, FLORIDA

# THE CHURCH THAT WILL MISS THE RAPTURE

## COLENE LEDFORD

CREATION
HOUSE
A STRANG COMPANY

THE CHURCH THAT WILL MISS THE RAPTURE
by Colene Ledford
Published by Creation House
A Strang Company
600 Rinehart Road
Lake Mary, Florida 32746
www.creationhouse.com

Unless otherwise noted, all Scripture quotations are from the King James Version of the Bible.

Cover design by Terry Clifton

Author photo by Anna Colene Rodgers

Library of Congress Control Number: 2005924886
International Standard Book Number: 1-59185-811-9

05 06 07 08 09 — 987654321

Printed in the United States of America

# CONTENTS

# INTRODUCTION

FOR MANY YEARS I have studied Bible prophecy, with prayer and fasting. And as I studied, the words began to come together like the pieces of a giant puzzle. And as they came together, they began to make the big picture of what God had planned for His children from the beginning of time. God's love for all His children is immeasurable, and He will do all that He can to bring as many of His children to Him, as will come. God knows that His children must be made aware, and be informed of the things that are to come upon the earth. Only then can they prepare fully and be ready when He comes in the clouds for His saints. Bible prophecy is being unsealed every day now, for we are truly living in the last days. We have an obligation to share any and all revelations that the Holy Spirit of God gives to anyone who studies God's Holy Word. In Hosea 4:6, we are told that "My people are destroyed for lack of knowledge." God is concerned that His children do not know all that they should concerning their lifetime spent here on earth.

There are three types of people here on earth: the godly, the ungodly, and the sinner. First Peter 4:18 poses the question: "And if the righteous scarcely be saved, where shall the ungodly and the sinner appear?" This book is based primarily on this question: If the righteous, or godly, scarcely be saved; why? And when they are raptured, where do the *ungodly* come in? Who are the *ungodly*? These are those who have been saved but have iniquity in their lives: unrepented sins. And of course, the sinners are those who have never acknowledged the Lord as Savior of their lives. There will be another group of people who will be counted among the sinners: those who have committed the unpardonable sin.

I have written this chapter, as well as the entire book, by the leading of God's Holy Spirit. My intentions are not to offend anyone, but to enlighten God's people to His Word. This chapter covers who can commit the unpardonable sin and how it is committed. That brings us to the chapter about the church that will miss the Rapture. The chapter will explain in detail who will be in that church and why. None of us want to be in that church. We want to be with those who go with the Lord in the Rapture. Let us be made aware of why they missed the Rapture and study the Scriptures together to find that answer. And last, but certainly not least, the chapter about God's chosen people, the Jews. They are a big part of the puzzle, and that makes the big picture of what all of this is about. God has a covenant with His chosen people, and He will keep this covenant with them. He loves them so much that He will do all that is necessary to save as many as possible and bring them back to their homeland. This will include the parting of the waters once again to bring them through on dry ground. It is in the Scriptures, and it will come to pass. God will fulfill His covenant with them. The revealing of how He will accomplish this is beautiful. May God's blessings be upon you and yours as you read this book and study God's Word.

# Chapter 1

# GOD WILL DO ALL
# THAT HE PLANNED TO DO

G OD HAD A plan from the beginning. He will do all that He planned to do. He is an awesome and almighty God. There is not, never was, and never will be one like Him. He reminds us of this in Isaiah:

> Remember the former things of old: for I am God, and there is none else; I am God, and there is none like me, Declaring the end from the beginning, and from ancient times the things that are not yet done, saying, My Counsel shall stand, and I will do all my pleasure.
>
> —ISAIAH 46:9–10

What is God's pleasure? What does God want? When we study His precious Word, the answer is plain: God simply wants children who will love Him, obey Him, want to be close to Him, be faithful to Him, and serve Him. From the beginning, He wanted only those who chose to love Him. He has never and will never force anyone to love Him. He made each of us in His likeness; we are free moral agents to make decisions on our own. We must choose to follow Him and to be His children. First, there were the angels; they had everything that God could give them to make them happy. But one-third of them rebelled against God and followed Lucifer. Lucifer was the archangel, second only to God Himself. But Lucifer became exalted and convinced one-third of God's angels to rebel against God. And, as we know, they are now in spiritual darkness, awaiting Judgment Day:

> For if God spared not the angels that sinned, but cast them down to hell, and delivered them into chains of darkness, to be reserved unto judgment; And spared not the old world, but saved Noah the eighth person, a preacher of righteousness, bringing in the flood upon the world of the ungodly; And turning the cities of Sodom and Gomorrah into ashes condemned them with an overthrow, making them as ensample unto those that after should live ungodly; And delivered just Lot, vexed with the filthy conversation of the wicked: (For that righteous man dwelling among them, in seeing and hearing, vexed his righteous soul from day to day with their unlawful deeds;) The Lord knoweth how to deliver the godly out of temptations, and to reserve the unjust unto the day of judgment to be punished.
>
> —2 PETER 2:4–9

God wants children who are godly and righteous, nothing less. He did not spare the angels that fell. He brought a flood upon the old world to destroy it, and He made an example out of Sodom and Gomorrah. And through it all, He delivered the godly. The unjust are kept until the Day of Judgment to be punished. God's aim is to have children who will choose to love Him unconditionally. After the angels fell, God decided to have children who were made in His image. Surely then, mankind would want to love and fellowship with Him. He placed Adam and Eve in a beautiful garden, furnished with all that they would ever need to be content and happy as they fellowshiped with Him. Surely, with all of that, they would choose to be godly. But God knew that they must be given the ability to choose, as well as to be tried and tested. We know that they failed the test, and the same day were shut out of the garden. The day that they sinned, they died spiritually. By woman, sin came into the garden, and by woman, God would take what Satan meant for evil and turn it into good:

> And I will put enmity between thee and the woman, and between thy seed and her seed; it shall bruise thy head, and thou shalt bruise his heal.
>
> —Genesis 3:15

Adam and Eve bore children and the earth became populated. But after two thousand years, God repented that He had even made man; because man was so wicked on the earth:

> And God saw that the wickedness of man was great in the earth, and that every imagination of the thoughts of his heart was only evil continually. And it repented the Lord that he had made man on the earth, and it grieved him at his heart. And the Lord said, I will destroy man whom I have created from the face of the earth; both man, and beast, and the creeping thing, and the fowls of the air; for it repenteth me that I have made them. But Noah found grace in the eyes of the Lord.
>
> —Genesis 6:5–8

So God spared Noah, his wife, his three sons, and their wives. We all know the story of how God told Noah to build an ark; to furnish it with food and necessities for his family, and all the animals, fowl, and creeping things that he would bring onto it. The rains came and destroyed all that was not in the ark. After forty days, the rains ceased; the waters dried up, and they came out of the ark. The first thing that Noah did was build an altar and offer burnt offerings unto God, of every fowl and beast that was clean. God was pleased and made a promise to all men:

> And the LORD smelled a sweet savour; and the LORD said in his heart, I will not again curse the ground any more for man's sake; for the imagination of man's heart is evil from his youth; neither will I again smite any more every thing living, as I have done.
>
> —GENESIS 8:21

> While the earth remaineth, seedtime and harvest, and cold and heat, and summer and winter, and day and night shall not cease.
>
> —GENESIS 8:22

Without the shedding of blood, there was no remission of sin. And just as God promised; two thousand years after the flood, Jesus was born of the Virgin Mary. Jesus walked this earth for thirty-three years; teaching, preaching, and healing the sick. God's plan, from the beginning, was that Jesus would be the sacrificial Lamb for the sins of the world. God loves us that much; that He would send His Son, His only Son, to be a sacrifice for our sins. Never again would burnt offerings of animals be necessary for us to receive pardon for our sins. God's promise to us is "that whosoever will may come":

> For God so loved the world, that he gave his only begotten Son, that whosoever believeth in him should not perish, but have everlasting life. For God sent not his Son into the world to condemn the world; but that the world through him might be saved.
>
> —JOHN 3:16–17

When God gave His Son, Jesus, as the sacrificial Lamb for our sins, He had done all that He could do to bring us back to Him. Each of us must make that choice; to follow Him and have everlasting life, or reject Him. God did not promise that it would always be easy, but He did promise that He would send His Holy Spirit to be our Comforter and our guide. John quoted Jesus in his gospel:

> But the Comforter, which is the Holy Ghost, whom the Father will send in my name, he shall teach you all things, and bring all things to your remembrance, whatsoever I have said unto you.
>
> —JOHN 14:26

God knew that all would be born into sin because of Adam and Eve, but we would not be condemned for that. We would only be condemned if we chose to reject Him as the Savior who was sacrificed for our sins. Jesus gave His life willingly on the cross so that all we had to do was repent of our sins, believe in the Lord, Jesus Christ, and receive Him into our heart. When you acknowledge this, you become a new creation with God's Holy Spirit living within you to lead and guide you. God's plan is to have children who love Him unconditionally and who are willing to be tried and tested. God will do all that He planned to do, and He will have children who love Him and want to be with Him throughout eternity.

# Chapter 2

# GOD'S WORD IS
# LIKE A JIGSAW PUZZLE

G OD HAS GIVEN us His precious Word to use as a road map as we make this journey through life here on earth. It is put together like a giant jigsaw puzzle, to make the big picture of all that God has planned for us. The Holy Bible was written by holy men of God as they were moved by the Holy Spirit of God:

> For the prophecy came not in old time by the will of man: but holy men of God spake as they were moved by the Holy Ghost.
>
> —2 PETER 1:21

And because it was written by holy men of God, moved upon by the Holy Ghost, it will only be understood fully by holy men or women of God, moved by the Holy Ghost. This is why we need preachers, teachers, and writers, moved by the Holy Ghost, to preach and to teach the Holy Bible. We must pray for wisdom and understanding, as we read and study His precious Word:

> My people are destroyed for lack of knowledge.
> —Hosea 4:6

We must change that. People should not perish because they do not know. We must share those truths that have been revealed to us by His Holy Spirit, even though it has never been taught by others. God's Word is our confirmation. Not one word was written in our Holy Bible by accident or coincidence, but rather by holy men of God, moved by the Holy Spirit. Every word fits and makes the big picture, like a giant jigsaw puzzle, containing what God wants to make known to those who know Him and love Him. Let us now study God's Word together and put the pieces of this giant puzzle into the right places. This will reveal the big picture that God wants us to see. Godly people should not perish for lack of knowledge. We know that there are three types of people on this earth: the godly, the ungodly, and the sinner.

The godly are those who are walking with the Lord and obeying His Word. The ungodly are those who have been saved but have iniquity or sin in their life. Of course, the sinner is one who has never acknowledged the Lord as Savior, nor asked Him to come into his heart. Peter poses the question, where will they appear at His coming?

> And if the righteous scarcely be saved, where shall the ungodly and the sinner appear?
> —1 Peter 4:18

This is the question that we will answer in this book, and also one that we should all ask ourselves: Would we be numbered with the godly, or the ungodly? God is no respecter of persons. Each one of us will give an account and be responsible for what we have done in our lifetimes unless it has been wiped from our record and is under the blood, in the Sea of Forgetfulness, never to be held against us again. Paul cautions us, in a letter to the Romans:

> For what if some did not believe? Shall their unbelief make the faith of God without effect? God forbid: yea, let God be true, but every man a liar; as it is written, That thou mightest be justified in thy sayings, and mightest overcome when thou art judged.
>
> —ROMANS 3:3–4

Let us now begin to make the big picture come together.

# Chapter 3

# PROPHECY

THE DEFINITION OF the word *prophecy* is "history in advance." There are eight thousand prophetic words in the Bible, and five thousand of them pertain to the coming of the Lord. Everyone is interested in prophecy and is anxious to know what God's Word says about future events. The Bible is the only accurate source that we have. We strive to find out all that we can concerning all the events that are destined to happen in the future of our world as we know it. Prophecy was written by holy men of God as they were moved by the Holy Spirit of God: but not always understood by those who wrote it. Daniel revealed to us in this next verse his concern and lack of understanding about the revelations that God was giving to him:

> And I heard, but I understood not: then said I, O my Lord, what shall be the end of these things? And he said,

Go thy way, Daniel: for the words are closed up and
sealed till the time of the end.

—Daniel 12:8–9

And now, because we do understand these words of prophecy, as well as all the other prophecies in God's Word, this must be "the time of the end." Prophecies in God's Word are being fulfilled every day. God told Daniel that knowledge would be increased at "the time of the end." Today, with the technology of the computer industry, is there any end to the increase of knowledge that we have at our disposal? We are truly living in the days of "the time of the end."

But thou, O Daniel, shut up the words, and seal the book,
even to the time of the end: many shall run to and fro,
and knowledge shall be increased.

—Daniel 12:4

We know now that we are living in "the time of the end," and the words that were closed up and sealed at that time are now being revealed every day to those who are seeking and searching God's Word to find the truths that are hidden therein. Now is the time to prayerfully study God's Word and pray for wisdom to understand all that God has in store for us and all mankind. And as you read this book and we study God's Word together, let us pray that we never get to the point that we feel that we know it all and cannot be taught something new. They who feel that way have a closed mind, and even the Spirit of God cannot teach them. They have their minds made up and do not want to be confused with the facts. Please read this book with an open mind and be willing to study the Scriptures for confirmation.

Let us begin with the times spoken of in the Bible. Peter

tells us that one day is with the Lord as a thousand years, and a thousand years as one day:

> But, beloved, be not ignorant of this one thing, that one day is with the Lord as a thousand years, and a thousand years as one day.
>
> —2 PETER 3:8

In many places in the Bible, reference is made to the phrase, "of that day," or, "in that day." In many instances the reference means "in that thousand years." The number seven is God's perfect number, the number of completion. This number is used extensively throughout the Bible. God has allotted seven thousand years to man on this earth to perfect and make ready those who desire to be His children for eternity. From Creation to Noah was two thousand years; from Noah to the birth of Christ was two thousand years; from the birth of Christ to the time of the Rapture will have been two thousand years; and the one thousand year, called the Millennium, will complete the seven thousand years, God's number of completion.

The Church Age began in the fifth day, on the Day of Pentecost. Paul gives all the details in Acts, chapter 2. We are now living in the sixth day, or the sixth thousandth year on God's calendar since Creation. We are now living in the last days of the six thousandth year. I will not compromise with those who say that the earth is millions of years old, or that man has been here on earth for an extended period of time. The God I serve can cause anything or anyone to look as old as He wills. My Bible says that seven thousand years have been allotted to man here on earth to prepare for eternity, and then time shall be no more. Where each of us will spend eternity is determined by how we live while we are here on earth. David describes our lifetime "as of grass, or a flower of the field" in Psalms:

> As for man, his days are as grass: as a flower of the field,
> so he flourisheth. For the wind passeth over it, and it is
> gone; and the place thereof shall know it no more.
>
> —Psalms 103:15–16

God placed within each of us a desire to know Him and to love Him. We are not fulfilled until God's Spirit lives within us and we are in His will. He loves us and wants us to be prepared to spend eternity with Him. To know Him is to love Him. God knew that we would have troubles and trials while we were here on earth, but there is comfort in His Word:

> Fret not thyself because of evildoers, neither be thou envious against the workers of iniquity. For they shall soon be cut down like the grass, and wither as the green herb. Trust in the Lord, and do good; so shalt thou dwell in the land, and verily thou shalt be fed. Delight thyself also in the Lord: and he shall give thee the desires of thine heart. Commit thy way unto the Lord; trust also in him; and he shall bring it to pass. And he shall bring forth thy righteousness as the light, and thy judgment as the noonday. Rest in the Lord, and wait patiently for him: fret not thyself because of him who prospereth in his way, because of the man who bringeth wicked devices to pass. Cease from anger, and forsake wrath: fret not thyself in any wise to do evil. For evildoers shall be cut off: but those that wait upon the Lord, they shall inherit the earth. For yet a little while, and the wicked shall not be: yea, thou shalt diligently consider his place, and it shall not be. But the meek shall inherit the earth; and shall delight themselves in the abundance of peace.
>
> —Psalms 37:1–11

18

Let us live each day as if it were our last one, and plan each day as if we will live forever. We have only our lifetime to prove ourselves worthy to be called the children of God. Let us not fail to perform this task so that our lifetime will be fulfilled in service to our Lord and Savior, Jesus Christ. I believe, as well as many others, that we are the generation that will be here on earth when the first resurrection and the Rapture of the saints will occur. We are living in the evening part of the sixth day, or six thousandth year. The Rapture, and then the seven years of tribulation, are yet to come in this six thousandth year. Then will come in the millennial reign with Christ here on earth, Satan being loosed for a season to try those who are on earth at that time, and then an eternity with our Lord. And time shall be no more. We are reminded of what God told Daniel:

> But go thou thy way till the end be: for thou shalt rest, and stand in thy lot at the end of the days.
> —DANIEL 12:13

> And he said, Go thy way, Daniel: for the words are closed up and sealed till the time of the end.
> —DANIEL 12:9

This is the time of the end, and God's prophetic words are being unsealed more and more each day. Knowledge has increased tremendously, just as God's Word told us that it would in the last days. We pray that we might stand in the lot with the righteous saints at the end of days, just as He told Daniel that He would. God also promised that He would reveal to us all things that were coming upon the earth. Amos, the prophet, said it well:

> Surely the Lord God will do nothing, but he revealeth his secret unto his servants the prophets.
>
> —Amos 3:7

And Paul, in the New Testament, explains it well:

> But ye, brethren, are not in darkness, that that day should overtake you as a thief. Ye are all the children of light, and the children of the day: we are not of the night, nor of darkness. Therefore let us not sleep, as do others; but let us watch and be sober. For they that sleep sleep in the night; and they that be drunken are drunken in the night. But let us, who are of the day, be sober, putting on the breastplate of faith and love; and for an helmet, the hope of salvation. For God hath not appointed us to wrath, but to obtain salvation by our Lord Jesus Christ, Who died for us, that, whether we wake or sleep, we would live together with him.
>
> —1 Thessalonians 5:4–10

And again, as Paul speaks to the Christians, he explains to us that only by the Spirit of God can we understand the Word of God:

> Now we have received, not the spirit of the world, but the spirit which is of God; that we might know the things that are freely given to us of God. Which things also we speak, not in the words which man's wisdom teacheth, but which the Holy Ghost teacheth; comparing spiritual things with spiritual. But the natural man receiveth not the things of the Spirit of God: for they are foolishness unto him: neither can he know them, because they are spiritually discerned. But he that is spiritual judgeth all things, yet he himself is judged of no man. For who hath

known the mind of the Lord, that he may instruct him?
But we have the mind of Christ.

—1 CORINTHIANS 2:12–16

My prayer is that you will allow the Spirit of God within you to reveal to you the truth as you read this book. His promise to us is that every prophecy will be fulfilled before the end of time:

> For verily I say unto you, Till heaven and earth pass, one jot or one tittle shall in no wise pass from the law, till all be fulfilled.

—MATTHEW 5:18

# Chapter 4

# THE DOOR

THE DOOR THAT I am referring to in this chapter is the *door* that is Jesus Christ. As we know, this door is the only door to salvation for any of us. John quoted Jesus in his Gospel, in Jesus' own words, that He is the door.

I am the door: by me if any man enter in, he shall be saved, and shall go in and out, and find pasture.

—JOHN 10:9

Jesus is the only door to salvation and eternal life. That door is open to all who will believe and receive Him as Lord of their life. This door is a big piece of the puzzle that we are putting together to make the big picture. This picture will show us what God has planned for us as we travel this road of life and prepare for Him coming in the clouds for His saints. Jesus is also the door to our Father God, as John once again quotes Him:

> Jesus saith unto him, I am the way, the truth, and the life:
> no man cometh unto the Father, but by me.
>
> —John 14:6

Jesus Christ is truly the only door to our salvation and the only door to our Father God. This door is open to whosoever will come, for now, but for how long? When we study God's Word, we find that this door is going to be closed. When will it close, who will close it, and why will it be closed? To answer those questions, we will begin with the parable that Jesus gave to us of the ten virgins:

> Then shall the kingdom of heaven be likened unto ten virgins, which took their lamps, and went forth to meet the bridegroom. And five of them were wise, and five were foolish. They that were foolish took their lamps, and took no oil with them: But the wise took oil in their vessels with their lamps. While the bridegroom tarried, they all slumbered and slept. And at midnight, There was a cry made, Behold, the bridegroom cometh; go ye out to meet him. Then all those virgins arose, and trimmed their lamps. And the foolish said unto the wise, Give us your oil; for our lamps are gone out. But the wise answered, saying, Not so; lest there be not enough for us and you: but go ye rather to them that sell, and buy for yourselves. And while they went to buy, the bridegroom came: and they that were ready went in with him to the marriage: and the door was shut. Afterward came also the other virgins, saying, Lord, Lord, open to us. But he answered and said, Verily I say unto you, I know you not. Watch and therefore, for ye know neither the day nor the hour wherein the Son of man cometh.
>
> —Matthew 25:1–13

This is a parable given to us by Jesus Christ Himself, of the first resurrection, and then the Rapture of the saints who are ready to meet Him. It is written to let us know that not all who come forth in the first resurrection will go with Him in the Rapture. In the parable, all ten of the women were virgins, which meant that all of them had been saved and had the Spirit of God in them, and had been in the kingdom of God since death. And because of this, they all heard the cry at midnight and came forth. All of them were looking and waiting for Jesus' return. Remember, Jesus used this parable to show us what would happen at the time of the first resurrection, which will be for only those who have the Spirit of God in them. With this parable, we see that only half of those who are expecting to go with Him in the Rapture will be ready to go when He does come. Once those who are ready are caught up with Him in the clouds, the door is shut.

But let us go back to those who will be changed or resurrected, given new bodies, and are here on earth. They will question the Lord as to why they were left out, and He will answer them. When we study God's Word, we find in many places that our garments of salvation must be white and clean, or we cannot enter into the kingdom of heaven. Those who will be left will have spots and blemishes on their robes of salvation. But all is not lost; because they have the Spirit of God in them, and their names are written in the Book of Life, they will have another chance. But they must go through the tribulations that are to come upon the earth. They must be tried and tested by fire. They must hold fast to their faith and their testimony of our Lord, Jesus Christ. More details are given in the chapter of Resurrection and Rapture in this book.

There were ten virgins, all saved, but only five of them had enough oil in their lamps, or Spirit of God in them, to go with the Lord when He came for them. They were all resurrected and given new bodies, but only five of them went with the Lord. Could that be the ratio of the ones taken and the ones left? That is the same ratio given in Matthew's Gospel, for those who are alive when Jesus returns for his saints.

> Then shall two be in the field; the one shall be taken, and the other left. Two women shall be grinding at the mill; the one shall be taken, and the other left.
>
> —MATTHEW 24:40-41

That would mean that only half of all of the Christians, whether they are dead or alive, who are expecting to go with the Lord in the Rapture will actually be able to go. That is a sobering thought. Do we have enough of the Spirit of God in us to be able to go with Him when He comes for us? We are cautioned many times in the Scriptures to be alert and to be ready, for we know neither the day nor the hour that the Son of Man will come. We are also cautioned that many will seek to enter in and not be able to. What do we have in our life that might keep us from being ready to go with Him? The word *iniquity* can cover a lot of things. Do we have iniquity in our lives?

Luke's Gospel has some sobering words on it:

> Strive to enter in at the strait gate: for many, I say unto you, will seek to enter in, and shall not be able. When once the master of the house has risen up, and hath shut to the door, and ye begin to stand without, and to knock at the door, saying, Lord, Lord, open unto us; and He shall answer and say unto you, I know you not whence ye are: Then shall ye begin to say, We have eaten and drunk in thy presence, and thou hast taught in our streets. But he shall say, I tell you, I know you not whence ye are; depart from me, all ye workers of iniquity. There shall be

weeping and gnashing of teeth, when ye shall see Abraham, and Isaac, and Jacob, and all the prophets, in the kingdom of God, and you yourselves thrust out.

—LUKE 13:24–28

When Jesus comes back to call forth all who have the Spirit of God in them at the first resurrection, all who are ready will be changed and will meet Him in the air. And then the door is shut. All others who have come forth at the same time will want to come in, but cannot. Jesus will tell them that it is because they have iniquity in their hearts, and He does not know them.

They will have been in the kingdom of God with all the old prophets since death. They will have enjoyed all that God had for them, in the kingdom of God; from the time that they died here on earth, and their spirit went to be with the Lord, until the day of the first resurrection. That will be the day of truth for all believers. If there are spots or blemishes on your robe of salvation, you will be thrust out of the kingdom of God and onto the earth. There, you must go through the time of tribulation that is to come upon the earth, to be tried and tested, and your robes made white. Luke leaves no question in our mind concerning this:

> There shall be weeping and gnashing of teeth, when ye shall see Abraham, and Isaac, and all the prophets, in the kingdom of God, and you yourselves thrust out.
>
> —LUKE 13:28

Can you imagine how you would feel if this happened to you? Wouldn't you be weeping and gnashing your teeth in disgust, because you had not stayed true to Him? Jesus always had a parable to help us understand the meanings in His precious Word:

Who then is a faithful and wise servant, whom his lord hath made ruler over his household, to give them meat in due season? Blessed is that servant, whom his lord when he cometh shall find so doing. Verily I say unto you, That he shall make him ruler over all his goods. But and if that evil servant shall say in his heart, My lord delayeth his coming; And shall begin to smite his fellowservants, and to eat and drink with the drunken; The lord of that servant shall come in a day when he looketh not for him, and in an hour that he is not aware of, And shall cut him asunder, and appoint him his portion with the hippocrites: there shall be weeping and gnashing of teeth.

—MATTHEW 24:45–51

Luke gave us the information on those who had died and gone on to the kingdom of God. Then at the time of the resurrection those who were not ready were cast out of the kingdom of God. The parable in Matthew denotes those who are alive when Jesus comes back in the clouds to gather His own, at the time of the first resurrection. Then they will realize that they will have been left here on earth to go through the tribulations that are to come to all who dwell on the earth. They must be tried and tested, to make their robes white, to enter into the kingdom of God. There is no other way, *the door has been shut.*

# Chapter 5

# RESURRECTION AND RAPTURE

As BELIEVERS, WE look forward to the day of the first resurrection and rapture of the saints of God. Paul's words give us comfort in knowing that we will not be ignorant or complacent as we see the time approaching for His coming. Whether it be by death and resurrection, or alive and being changed in the twinkling of an eye, we must have on our armor of faith, love, and the hope of salvation. We must be ready when He comes. How we live while we are here on earth will determine our destiny for eternity.

> But of the times and the seasons, brethren, ye have no need that I write unto you. For yourselves know perfectly that the day of the Lord so cometh as a thief in the night. For when they shall say, Peace and safety; then sudden

destruction cometh upon them, as travail upon a woman with child; and they shall not escape. But ye, brethren, are not in darkness, that that day should overtake you as a thief. Ye are all the children of the day: we are not of the night, nor of darkness. Therefore let us not sleep, as do others; but let us watch and be sober. For they that sleep in the night; and they that be drunken are drunken in the night. But let us, who are of the day, be sober, putting on the breastplate of faith and love; and for an helmet, the hope of salvation. For God hath not appointed us to wrath, but to obtain salvation by our Lord Jesus Christ, Who died for us, that, whether we wake or sleep, we should live together with him.

—1 THESSALONIANS 5:1–10

God wants us to be prepared when our time comes, whether by death or the first resurrection and rapture. Paul tells us, as believers, that to be absent from the body is to be present with the Lord (2 Corinthians 5:8). As believers, when our bodies die here on earth, our souls go to be with the Lord in the kingdom of God. All who were saved in their lifetimes and believed in the Lord Jesus Christ as their Savior will be there together, from all the Church Ages. It is a beautiful place; we know because the Bible tells us so. We realize, as we study God's Word that this is the kingdom of God. This is the part of heaven where all of the dead in Christ are gathered together. They are also waiting for the first resurrection, when they will be changed in the twinkling of an eye. Let us see what Paul says in 1 Corinthians:

Behold, I shew you a mystery; We shall not all sleep, but we shall all be changed, In a moment, in the twinkling of an eye, at the last trump: for the trumpet shall sound, and the dead shall be raised incorruptible, and we shall be changed.

—1 CORINTHIANS 15:51–52

This promise to all believers is repeated many times in God's holy Word. Let us read what John had to say when he quoted Jesus:

> Verily, verily, I say unto you, The hour is coming, and now is, when the dead shall hear the voice of the Son of God: and they that hear shall live. Marvel not at this: for the hour is coming, in the which all that are in the graves shall hear his voice, And shall come forth; they that have done good, unto the resurrection of life; and they that have done evil, unto the resurrection of damnation.
>
> —JOHN 5:25, 28–29

In Jesus' own words, He is telling us that all will hear His voice and will come forth in their own time. We know that there will be two resurrections: the first will be for all believers. They will hear His voice, come forth, be changed in the twinkling of an eye, and have new bodies. The second resurrection will not occur until after the thousand-year reign with Christ, with the saints here on earth. Again, Jesus will call forth the dead and all sinners from all the ages will hear His voice and come forth. They will also be changed and given new bodies, to stand before almighty God, to be judged for their deeds and sentenced to eternal damnation in the lake of fire.

> But the rest of the dead lived not again until the thousand years were finished.
>
> —REVELATION 20:5

Paul gives us a beautiful rendition of what the rapture of the saints will be like:

> For the Lord himself shall descend from heaven with a shout, with the voice of the archangel, and with the trump of God: and the dead in Christ shall rise first: Then we which are alive and remain shall be caught up together with them in the clouds to meet the Lord in the air: and so shall we ever be with the Lord.
>
> —1 Thessalonians 4:16–17

The Lord shall call forth the dead in Christ, first, with a shout. The voice of the archangel will summon the living, and the trumpet of God will assemble the saints together. Those who are ready, whose garments of salvation are white and clean, will meet the Lord in the air to be with Him forever throughout eternity. These are God's promises to us, to which we can look forward, as we walk this road of life. But let us not become anxious or ahead of ourselves. As much as we want to believe that Jesus could come at any moment—and He could come for us by death, at any time—we are talking about the Rapture. We must study His Word and pray for God to give us wisdom to understand and to know the signs of His coming. He does not want us to be asleep or ignorant of the things that are coming to pass. We are living in the last days. The prophecies surrounding His coming are being fulfilled every day. But Paul cautions us not to be misled concerning Jesus' return for His saints:

> Now we beseech you, brethren, by the coming of our Lord Jesus Christ, and by our gathering together unto him, That ye be not soon shaken in mind, or be troubled, neither by spirit, nor by word, nor by letter as from us, as that the day of Christ is at hand. Let no man deceive you by any means: for that day shall not come, except there

come a falling away first, and that man of sin be revealed,
the son of perdition.

—2 THESSALONIANS 2:1–3

Paul is cautioning us not to be misled by any man if his
words do not line up with God's Word: the Day of the Lord
will not come until first there is a great falling away of the faith.
We are witnessing a growing resistance to the Christian faith
and the Word of God. The posting of the Ten Commandments
in prominent places has become an issue in many parts of our
country. There are also those who want to take the words "In
God We Trust" off our currency. Even the words "Under God"
in our Pledge of Allegiance to our flag, are under attack. There
is definitely a growing resentment against the Christian faith
in our country today. There is also an ever-growing number of
people who do not attend church. Even so, there is a growing
Christian faith movement worldwide.

We are seeing some of the greatest revivals in the history of
the church. Many of our evangelists are being allowed to go to
countries that have never heard the gospel and lead people to
the saving knowledge of the Lord Jesus. We have the greatest
communication systems now to transmit the gospel all over
the world. Literally thousands of people are coming to the saving knowledge of Christ every day. We are witnessing, in our
lifetime, God's Word preached around the world for a witness
to all nations. In Jesus' own words, He gave us this promise
and was quoted by Matthew:

And this gospel of the kingdom shall be preached in all
the world for a witness unto all nations; and then shall
the end come.

—MATTHEW 24:14

We know by Jesus' own words that we are truly living in the last days. But where are we in those last days? Paul told us that there would be a falling away of the faith before Jesus would come back for us. We are still enjoying this mighty move of God here on earth, and of course we would like it to stay that way. But God's Word tells us that it will not. Every day, we see all mention of God being taken away from one thing or another. Taking prayer out of our schools was one of the worst things that could have happened. Now we have a discipline problem with our children. Not only that, but many children never hear any words from the Bible because of this. As God is taken out of more and more things pertaining to the general public, we will see more and more evil abound. God is being taken out of all that might convict a sinner of his wrongdoing. This, in time, will be a cause of the falling away of the faith. There is no vacuum in the spiritual world; as God is taken out of our midst, Satan will replace that void and fill it. We must work for the Lord while we can, for the night will come, and then the falling away of the faith, when no man can work. These are Jesus' own words, recorded by John, and this reference is letting us know that spiritual darkness will cover the earth before He comes back for His saints:

> I must work the works of him that sent me, while it is day: the night cometh, when no man can work.
> —JOHN 9:4

On God's timetable, the midnight hour will be the darkest, spiritually darkest, hour ever to be, for His saints. But this will also be the time that He will return for them:

> And at midnight there was a cry made, Behold the bride-
> groom cometh; go ye out to meet him.
>
> —MATTHEW 25:6

This doesn't mean that it would be midnight our time; this means that midnight in God's eyes will be the darkest time here on earth for the saints. This will surely be a dark time for Christians. We are not there yet, but we can see the signs of it coming. Also, the man of sin must be revealed: the Antichrist. That is the way that he will come on the scene: as a savior of the world, true to his name, the Antichrist. We may not recognize him at the beginning because he will come as a peacemaker. Seemingly, he will have all the answers to all the world's problems.

> And in the latter time of their kingdom, when the trans-
> gressors are come to the full, a king of fierce counte-
> nance, and understanding dark sentences, shall stand
> up And his power shall be mighty, but not by his own
> power: and he shall destroy wonderfully, and shall pros-
> per, and practise, and shall destroy the mighty and the
> holy people And through his policy also he shall cause
> craft to prosper in his hand; and he shall magnify him-
> self in his heart, and by peace shall destroy many: he
> shall also stand up against the Prince of princes; but he
> shall be broken without hand.
>
> —DANIEL 8:23–25

This man of sin will come from the European Economic Community. This is an organization that has been formed in Europe, with its headquarters in Rome, no less; by the heads-of-state of many countries from around the world. We who study Bible prophecy began to see how this organization was living up to Daniel's prophecies. Of course, we expected there to be ten nations, but at last count there are fifteen. But true to God's Word, I'm sure there will only be ten when the Antichrist is selected as their leader. Even now we are reading and hearing in the news that some of the nations are coming out of the alliance with the EEC. Now let us go to the Book of Daniel and see how all of this comes together. It begins with Daniel telling King Nebuchadnezzar what his dream was, and then the interpretation of his dream:

> Thou, O king, sawest, and behold a great image. This great image, whose brightness was excellent, stood before thee; and the form thereof was terrible. This image's head was of fine gold, his breast and his arms of silver, his belly and his thighs of brass, his legs of iron, his feet part of iron and part of clay. Thou sawest till that a stone was cut out without hands, which smote the image upon his feet that were of iron and clay, and break them to pieces. Then was the iron, the clay, the brass, the silver, and the gold, broken to pieces together, and became like the chaff of the summer threshing floors; and the wind carried them away, that no place was found for them: and the stone that smote the image became a great mountain, and filled the whole earth. This is the dream; and we will tell the interpretation thereof before the king. Thou, O king, art a king of kings: for the God of heaven hath given thee a kingdom, power, and strength, and glory. And wheresoever the children of men dwell, the beasts of the field and the fowls of the heaven hath he given into thine hand, and hath made thee ruler over them all. Thou art this head of gold. And after thee shall arise another kingdom inferior to thee, and another third kingdom of brass, which shall bear rule over all the earth. And the fourth kingdom shall be strong as iron: forasmuch as iron breaketh in pieces and subdueth all things: and as

iron that breaketh all these, shall it break in pieces and bruise. And whereas thou sawest the feet and toes, part of potters' clay, and part of iron, the kingdom shall be divided; but there shall be in it of the strength of iron, forasmuch as thou sawest the iron mixed with miry clay. And as the toes of the feet were part of iron, and part of clay, so the kingdom shall be partly strong, and partly broken. And whereas thou sawest iron mixed with miry clay, they shall mingle themselves with the seed of men: but they shall not cleave on to another, even as iron is not mixed with clay. And in the days of these kings shall the God of heaven set up a kingdom, which shall never be destroyed: and the kingdom shall not be left to other people, but it shall break in pieces and consume all these kingdoms, and it shall stand forever.

—DANIEL 2:31–44

Daniel's words reveal to us that there would be four empires that would rule the world: the Babylonian, Medo-Persian, Grecian, and Roman. The Roman Empire was the legs and feet in King Nebuchadnezzar's dream, and then there were the toes. Daniel said the kingdom would be divided (Dan. 2:41). This division would be by time itself. The first Roman Empire was from 753 B.C. to 1453. The Roman Empire represented by the ten toes will be reigning when our God comes back to earth to set up His kingdom (Dan. 2:44).

Now let us see where the Antichrist comes into this picture. Daniel had a night vision and was given this interpretation:

Thus he said, The fourth beast shall be the fourth kingdom upon earth, which shall be diverse from all kingdoms, and shall devour the whole earth, and shall tread it down, and break it in pieces. And the ten horns out of this kingdom are ten kings that shall arise: and another shall rise after them; and he shall be diverse from the first, and he shall subdue three kings. And he shall speak great words against the most High, and shall wear out the saints of the most High, and think to change times and laws: and they shall be given into his hand until a time and times and the dividing of time. But the judgment shall sit, and they shall take away his dominion, to consume and to destroy it unto the end. And the kingdom and dominion, and the greatness of the kingdom under the whole heaven, shall be given to the people of the saints of the most High, whose kingdom is an everlasting kingdom, and all dominions shall serve and obey him.

—DANIEL 7:23–28

With these scriptures you can see how the Antichrist will come on the scene and how he will be involved with the European Economic Community. This organization is in the process now of having a one-world government and a one-world currency. We have been hearing of this now for quite some time. The currency has already been printed. As the economies of the world keep getting worse, they will eventually sell out to the EEC.

John also prophesied the coming of the Antichrist, and aligns with Daniel's prophecy. (See Revelation 13:1–8.)

The world will accept the Antichrist because he seems to have all the answers to the world's problems. But as time goes on, things only get worse. That will be when the children of God begin to cry out and pray for the Lord's return. Only then will He hear our cries and prayers and come back for us. Luke quotes Jesus:

And shall not God avenge his own elect, which cry day and night unto him, though he bear long with them? I tell you that he will avenge them speedily. Nevertheless when the Son of man cometh, shall he find faith on the earth?

—LUKE 18:7–8

God will not deliver His people until they begin to cry out to Him for deliverance. When the children of Israel were in bondage in Egypt, He did not send Moses to deliver them until they began to cry unto Him. We will read that in Exodus:

> And it came to pass in process of time, that the king of Egypt died: and the children of Israel sighed by reason of the bondage, and they cried, and their cry came up unto God by reason of the bondage. And God heard their groaning, and God remembered his covenant with Abraham, with Isaac, and with Jacob. And God looked upon the children of Israel, and God had respect unto them.
>
> —EXODUS 2:23–25

Christians are not yet crying and praying for the Lord to deliver them; they are satisfied with the way things are now. But most things will change. We are now in the late evening part of the last day. Terrorism continues to strike unsuspecting targets around the world. Israel is being pounded daily, killing innocent people. The day will come when Jerusalem will be surrounded with armies:

> And when ye shall see Jerusalem compassed with armies, then know that the desolation thereof is nigh.
>
> —LUKE 21:20

Daniel chapter 12 gives us an insight of what things will be like for the House of Israel at the time of the coming of the Lord for His saints; these are his prophetic words:

> And at that time shall Michael stand up, the great prince
> which standeth for the children of thy people: and there
> shall be a time of trouble, such as never was since there
> was a nation even to that same time: and at that time thy
> people shall be delivered, every one that shall be found
> written in the book. And many of them that sleep in the
> dust of the earth shall awake, some to everlasting life,
> and some to shame and everlasting contempt.
>
> —DANIEL 12:1-2

Daniel is prophesying in the year of 534 B.C. of things that will come to pass just before the coming of the Lord, and of the coming of the Lord. This prophecy was for the house of Israel. He predicted the first resurrection. God also promised to put His Spirit in the whole house of Israel so that they would all be in the first resurrection. Ezekiel was told by Almighty God that this prophecy was for the whole house of Israel; that they would be resurrected, God would put His Spirit in them, and they would live and return to their homeland:

> Then he said unto me, Son of man, these bones are the
> whole house of Israel: behold they say, Our bones are
> dried, and our hope is lost: we are cut off for our parts.
> Therefore prophesy and say unto them, Thus saith the
> Lord God; Behold, O my people, I will open your graves,
> and cause you to come up out of your graves, and bring
> you into the land of Israel. And ye shall know that I am
> the LORD, when I have opened your graves, And shall
> put my spirit in you, and ye shall live, and I shall place
> you in your own land: then shall ye know that I the LORD
> have spoken it, and performed it, saith the Lord.
>
> —EZEKIEL 37:11-14

Paul told us of this in Romans 11:25-27:

For I would not, brethren, that ye should be ignorant of this mystery, lest ye should be wise in your own conceits; that blindness in part has happened to Israel, until the fullness of the Gentiles be come in. And so all Israel shall be saved: as it is written, There shall come out of Sion the Deliverer, and shall turn away ungodliness from Jacob: For this is my covenant unto them, when I shall take away their sins.

This is God's promise to the whole house of Israel: that they would be resurrected, given new bodies, and put in their own land, and without a doubt, they would know that He was almighty God when He put his Spirit into them. The house of Israel had been blinded by almighty God because of their transgressions. Many had died with no hope for their eternal souls. Their hope was gone, and they believed that they were cut off forever. But God had a covenant with them; they are His chosen people, the apple of His eye. He will never forsake them.[1]

This is the seed that was planted in my spirit many years ago, as I read these words. That is exactly what we have been saying will happen at the time of the first resurrection. All whose robes are white and clean will meet the Lord in the air. The Gentiles who have spots and blemishes on their robes of salvation will be left behind to be tried and tested.

Paul writes in his letter to the Ephesians what God expects of the church that will be ready to meet Him in the air:

[1]The word dwell, in Greek translation, which is used in the phrase, "Those who dwell upon the earth," in Revelation 3:10; 6:10; 11:10 and others, is not the same word in Greek as the ordinary word for dwell, in other places in the Bible. The ordinary word for dwell in Greek is oikeo, which means "to inhabit." But the Greek word for dwell used in Revelation, after the resurrection and rapture, is katoikeo. This word means "those who have settled down upon the earth, and have identified themselves with it." This information is from "Lectures in Systematic Theology," *Evangelical Commentary* (Cleveland, TN: Pathway Press, 1978).

> Husbands, love your wives, even as Christ also loved the church, and gave himself for it; That he might sanctify and cleanse it with the washing of water by the word, That he might present it to himself a glorious church, not having spot, or wrinkle, or any such thing; but that it should be holy and without blemish.
>
> —EPHESIANS 5:25–27

We know that there will be a great multitude who will be left here on earth; to be tried, tested, and then killed for their testimony. We know this because John told us about them in Revelation:

> After this I beheld, and lo, a great multitude, which no man could number, of all nations, and kindreds, and people, and tongues, stood before the throne, and before the Lamb, clothed with white robes, and palms in their hands; And cried with a loud voice, saying, Salvation to our God which sitteth upon the throne, and unto the Lamb. And all the angels stood round about the throne, and about the elders and the four beasts, and fell before the throne on their faces, and worshipped God, Saying, Amen: Blessing, and glory, and wisdom, and thanksgiving, and honor, and power, and might, be unto our God for ever and ever. Amen. And one of the elders answered, saying unto me, What are these which are arrayed in white robes? and whence came they? And I said unto him, Sir, thou knowest. And he said to me, These are they which came out of great tribulation, and have washed their robes, and made them white in the blood of the Lamb. Therefore are they before the throne of God, and serve him day and night in his temple: and he that sitteth on the throne shall dwell among them. They shall hunger no more, neither thirst any more; neither shall the sun light on them, nor any heat. For the Lamb which is

in the midst of the throne shall feed them, and shall lead them unto living fountains of waters: and God shall wipe away all tears from their eyes.

—REVELATION 7:9–11, 14–17

"A great multitude, that no man could number" will number more than those who are alive at the time of Jesus' return for His saints. It is a known fact that all who are alive today are numbered by census, in all nations of the world. Therefore, we know that this multitude that no man could number will include all saints who were not ready to meet the Lord in the air at the time of the first resurrection. This multitude will be dating back to the time of Noah's descendants, and up to the time that Jesus calls forth all saints in the first resurrection. That will be a number that "no man can number." Also, all who are resurrected will be made alive. Let us read that in 1 Corinthians:

> For since by man came death, by man came also the resurrection of the dead. For as in Adam all die, even so in Christ shall all be made alive. But every man in his own order: Christ the firstfruits; afterward they that are Christ's at his coming.
>
> —1 CORINTHIANS 15:21–23

All who are Christ's at His coming will be resurrected. That includes all who have the Spirit of God in them. The parable of the ten virgins is another good example (Matt. 25:1–13). All who have the Spirit of God in them will come forth when the cry is made (Matt. 25:6), but if there is not enough oil, or the Spirit of God in them, they will not meet Him in the air. Instead, it is obvious that they are left here on earth in their new bodies. In Luke's gospel, he called them "workers of iniquity":

> Strive to enter in at the strait gate: for many, I say unto
> you, will seek to enter in, and shall not be able. When
> once the master of the house is risen up, and hath
> shut to the door, and ye begin to stand without, and
> to knock at the door, saying, Lord, Lord, open unto
> us; and he shall answer and say unto you, I know you
> not whence ye are. Then shall ye begin to say, We have
> eaten and drunk in thy presence, and thou hast taught
> in our streets. But he shall say, I tell you, I know you
> not whence ye are; depart from me, all ye workers of
> iniquity. There shall be weeping and gnashing of teeth,
> when ye shall see Abraham, and Isaac, and Jacob, and
> all the prophets, in the kingdom of God, and you your-
> selves thrust out.
>
> —LUKE 13:24–28

So you see, you can be saved and still not be ready to meet
Him in the air. If you are not ready, you will go into the tribulation. But, hopefully, you will be one of the multitude who
will stand before the throne of God with white robe and palms
in your hands (Rev. 7:9).

And as we know, God will raise up the whole house of Israel,
put His Spirit in them, and lead them back to the homeland of
their forefathers. Regardless of where they might have lived,
during their lifetime, they shall be returned to Israel. Now let
us look at the first resurrection as it was revealed to John, the
Revelator. He begins with a blessing from almighty God, for
all those who "would die in the LORD; from henceforth."

> Here is the patience of the saints: here are they that keep
> the commandments of God, and the faith of Jesus. And I
> heard a voice from heaven saying unto me, Write, Blessed
> are the dead which die in the Lord from henceforth: Yea,

saith the Spirit, that they may rest from their labours; and their works do follow them.

—REVELATION 14:12–13

These are those who would give their lives for their testimony during the tribulations period, after the catching away of the saints.

Then we see in the next three verses the first part of the first resurrection. This part will include all who have the Spirit of God in them, Gentile and Jew. Both the living and the dead will come forth at the cry of our Lord and Savior, Jesus Christ. They will all be changed in the twinkling of an eye. Those who are ready to meet the Lord in the air will be given immortal bodies. But those who are left behind because of iniquity in their lives will be given new bodies and new life, and then left here to be tried and tested during the tribulations that are to come to all who dwell upon the earth. Scripture has this to say:

> And I looked, and behold a white cloud, and upon the cloud one sat like unto the Son of man, having on his head a golden crown, and in his hand a sharp sickle. And another angel came out of the temple, crying with a loud voice to him that sat on the cloud, Thrust in they sickle, and reap: for the time is come for thee to reap; for the harvest of the earth is ripe. And he that sat on the cloud thrust in his sickle on the earth; and the earth was reaped.
>
> —REVELATION 14:14–16

Jesus will be on that white cloud with a golden crown on His head, with a sickle in His hand, and the earth will be reaped. All who have the Spirit of God in them will be reaped. Now let us go to the second part of the first resurrection that John saw:

> And another angel came out of the temple which is in heaven, he also having a sharp sickle. And another angel came out from the altar, which had power over fire; and cried with a loud cry to him that had the sharp sickle, saying, Thrust in thy sharp sickle, and gather the clusters of the vine of the earth; for her grapes are fully ripe. And the angel thrust in his sickle into the earth, and gathered the vine of the earth, and cast it into the great winepress of the wrath of God. And the winepress was trodden without the city, and blood came out of the winepress, even unto the horse bridles, by the space of a thousand and six hundred furlongs.
>
> —REVELATION 14:17–20

In this part of the first resurrection we note that it was an angel who had the sharp sickle, and not Jesus. But there was also a second angel, one who had power over fire. This angel over fire had to give the order to the first angel to "thrust in the sickle and reap." We know that Jesus is the vine, so the clusters of the vine are none else but His chosen people, the Jews. They will literally be brought back from the gates of hell; hence the necessity of the angel over fire. This part of the first resurrection must be separate because this group will not have the Spirit of God in them until after they are raised up:

> And ye shall know that I am the LORD, when I have opened your graves, O my people, and brought you up out of your graves, And shall put my spirit in you, and ye shall live, and I shall place you in your own land: then shall ye know that I the LORD have spoken it, and performed it, saith the LORD.
>
> —EZEKIEL 37:13–14

And with this group, there are no exceptions; all will go through the tribulations as they dwell here on earth. God wanted them to know that they would be here on earth during the battle of Armageddon, which will be fought during the time of the tribulations (Rev. 14:19–20). Isaiah also prophesied the resurrection of the house of Israel and "his body":

> Thy dead men shall live, together with my dead body shall they arise. Awake and sing, ye that dwell in the dust: for thy dew is as the dew of herbs, and the earth shall cast out the dead. Come, my people, enter thou into thy chambers, and shut thy doors about thee: hide thyself as it were for a little moment, until the indignation be overpast. For, behold, the Lord cometh out of his place to punish the inhabitants of the earth for their iniquity: the earth also shall disclose her blood, and shall no more cover her slain.
>
> —Isaiah 26:19–21

The Lord is talking to the house of Israel, His chosen people. He is assuring them that they will be resurrected with His body, which is the church. But they must be prepared to go through the tribulations, or indignation along with those who have iniquity in their lives. Even so, they are His chosen people, and He promises to take care of them. He has a covenant with them, and that covenant will not be broken. Even so, all must be tried and tested, as by fire, and ultimately, give their lives for their testimony. But we remember the blessing that God gave to those who "die in the Lord from henceforth." This will be the second death, and it will not hurt them:

> Blessed and holy is he that hath part in the first resurrection: on such the second death hath no power, but they

shall be priests of God and of Christ, and shall reign with
him a thousand years.

—Revelation 20:6

Many of these who are resurrected will have been in the
kingdom of God, since death. I'm sure they are content and
happy to be there. That is what all Christians look forward to.
After this earthly body expires; to be in the kingdom of God,
and to be reunited with loved ones who have gone on before
us. And also, to be able to be there with all the Old Testament
prophets will be joy unspeakable. But what if there are spots
and wrinkles on your robe of salvation? You had accepted the
Lord Jesus as your Lord and Savior in your lifetime; you had
died and were in the kingdom of God rejoicing. And then the
cry is made for the first resurrection. At that time you will be
cast out of the kingdom of God, back onto earth in your new
body. Then would come the realization of what you should
have done in your lifetime that you did not do to be ready:

There shall be weeping and gnashing of teeth, when ye shall
see Abraham, and Isaac, and Jacob, and all the prophets,
in the kingdom of God, and you yourselves thrust out.

—Luke 13:28

To be "thrust out" would mean only one thing—that is
thrust out onto the earth to go through the tribulation. You
must wash your robe white by overcoming, and the word of
your testimony:

He that overcometh, the same shall be clothed in white
raiment; and I will not blot out his name out of the book
of life, but I will confess his name before my Father, and
before his angels.

—Revelation 3:5

That is what the Lord requires from each of us, that our robes of salvation are white and clean with no spots to be able to reign a thousand years with Him and to be with Him throughout eternity. They must overcome the Antichrist by their testimony, and by giving their lives for it:

> And they overcame him by the blood of the Lamb, and by the word of their testimony; and they loved not their lives unto the death.
>
> —REVELATION 12:11

> Husbands, love your wives, even as Christ also loved the Church, and gave himself for it; That he might sanctify and cleanse it with the washing of water by the word, That he might present it to himself a glorious church, not having spot, or wrinkle, or any such thing; but that it should be holy and without blemish.
>
> —EPHESIANS 4:25–28

For the house of Israel, God's chosen people, there will be no exceptions. First, all of them will be resurrected or changed, at the first resurrection. For all who are not ready to meet the Lord in the air, God's Spirit will be put into each one of them, and they will be led back to their father's homeland. This is God's covenant with the whole house of Israel, that all will be saved and given a second chance to call upon the name of the Lord and prepare for eternity.

> And so all Israel shall be saved: as it is written, There shall come out of Sion the Deliverer, and shall turn away ungodliness from Jacob: For this is my covenant unto them, when I shall take away their sins.
>
> —ROMANS 11:26–27

This is another exception that is afforded only to the house of Israel, God's chosen people. During the tribulations here on earth for God's chosen people, who will be in Mount Zion and Jerusalem, all who call upon the name of Lord shall be saved:

> The sun shall be turned into darkness, and the moon into blood, before the great and terrible day of the Lord come. And it shall come to pass, that whosoever shall call on the name of the Lord shall be delivered: for in mount Zion and in Jerusalem shall be deliverance, as the Lord hath said, and in the remnant whom the Lord shall call.
>
> —Joel 2:31–32

This scripture pertains only to God's chosen people during the time of great tribulations here on earth and in Zion and Jerusalem. This scripture will not apply to the Gentiles. They must have the Spirit of God within them to be able to be in the first resurrection. For God's chosen people, this will be the seventieth week that was promised to them by almighty God. But let us not get ahead of ourselves. Let us go back to Daniel's prophecy for more of what he had to say and prophesy about the Rapture:

> And many of them that sleep in the dust of the earth shall awake, some to everlasting life, and some to shame and everlasting contempt. Many shall be purified, and made white, and tried; but the wicked shall do wickedly: and none of the wicked shall understand; but the wise shall understand.
>
> —Daniel 12:2, 10

This is the first resurrection of the whole house of Israel. God was rejected by the Jews, and He turned to the Gentiles to get a bride. When the Spirit of God turned to the Gentiles, the eyes of the Jews were blinded to the gospel of Christ. They will be until God is finished with the Gentiles.

> For I would not, brethren, that ye should be ignorant of this mystery, lest ye should be wise in your own conceits; that blindness in part has happened to Israel, until the fulness of the Gentiles be come in.
>
> —ROMANS 11:25

John explained the plight of the house of Israel well in his gospel:

> But though he had done so many miracles before them, yet they believed not on him: That the saying of Esaias the prophet might be fulfilled, which he spake, Lord, who hath believed our report? And to whom hath the arm of the Lord been revealed? Therefore they could not believe, because that Esaias said again, He hath blinded their eyes and hardened their heart; that they should not see with their eyes, nor understand with their heart, and be converted, and I should heal them.
>
> —JOHN 12:37–40 (SEE ALSO ISAIAH 6:9–10)

That time will be at the first resurrection. Then God's Holy Spirit turns to the Jews, and with it they are resurrected, given new bodies, and are led back to their homeland. The seven years that follow are the seven years promised to the house of Israel, which is the seventieth week, spoken of by Daniel, the prophet. Paul's words in Romans 11 explain the plight of the Jews; we will go over just a part of it:

> And David saith, Let their table be made a snare, and a trap, and a stumblingblock, and a recompense unto them: Let their eyes be darkened, that they may not see,

and bow down their back away. I say then, Have they stumbled that they should fall? God forbid: but rather through their fall salvation is come unto the Gentiles, for to provoke them to jealousy. Now if the fall of them be the riches of the world, and the diminishing of them the riches of the Gentiles; how much more their fullness? For I speak to you Gentiles, in as much as I am the apostle of the Gentiles, I magnify mine office: If by any means I may provoke to emulation them which are my flesh, and might save some of them. For if the casting away of them be the reconciling of the world, what shall the receiving of them be, but life from the dead?

—ROMANS 11:9–15

For I would not, brethren, that ye should be ignorant of this mystery, lest ye should be wise in your own conceits, that blindness in part is happened to Israel, until the fulness of the Gentiles be come in. And so all Israel shall be saved: as it is written, There shall come out of Sion the Deliverer, and shall turn away ungodliness from Jacob: For this is my covenant unto them, when I shall take away their sins.

—ROMANS 11:25–27

This is exactly what we were talking about in reference to Ezekiel 37. It will be as life from the dead; all Israel will be saved, and He will take away their sins. That is His covenant with them. There are and were many Jews who have received Jesus Christ as their Messiah. And those whose robes of salvation are white and clean will be raptured when Jesus comes in the clouds to receive us unto Him.

But for all the house of Israel who were "blinded until the fulness of the Gentiles be come in" (Rom 11:25), they will be in the first resurrection. They will be given new bodies, new life, and God's Spirit will be put into them (Ezek. 37:12–14). He will also help them return to their homeland. And there they will go through the seven-year tribulation, known to the Jews as the "seventieth week of Daniel."

A summary of the seventy weeks that are allotted for His holy people and the holy city of Jerusalem is found in Daniel. This includes the time when our Lord will be proclaimed and anointed as the most Holy God:

> Seventy weeks are determined upon thy people and upon thy holy city, to finish the transgression and to make an end of sins, and to make reconciliation for iniquity, and to bring in everlasting righteousness, and to seal up the vision and prophecy, and to anoint the most Holy. Know therefore and understand, that from the going forth of the commandment to restore and to build Jerusalem unto the Messiah the Prince shall be seven weeks, and threescore and two weeks: the street shall be built again, and the wall, even in troublous times.
>
> —DANIEL 9:24–25

When we read the next verse, we see that sixty-two weeks of the seventy weeks ended when Jesus was crucified. This is the seventieth week promised to the Jews. It is their second chance to make heaven their home. They must be tried and tested, as by fire, and their robes made white and clean.

> And after threescore and two weeks shall Messiah be cut off, but not for himself: and the people of the prince that shall come shall destroy the city and the sanctuary; and the end thereof shall be with a flood, and unto the end of the war desolations are determined.
>
> —DANIEL 9:26

We know that when Jesus died on the cross, it was not for Himself but for all the sins of mankind. He paid the ultimate price, giving His life as the sacrificial Lamb for each one of us. The veil in the temple was torn from the top to the bottom when Jesus died on the cross for our sins. Never again would it be necessary to shed the blood of animals for the remission of sins. Jesus paid the price for our sins forever. All that we must do is to believe, repent, and receive. The prince who shall come will be the Antichrist. He and his armies will destroy the city of Jerusalem and the sanctuary, but not until after he has made a covenant or treaty with the Jews, for a period of seven years.

> And when ye shall see Jerusalem compassed with armies, then know that the desolation thereof is nigh.
> —Luke 21:20

But, after three and a half years, he breaks the treaty with them and desecrates the temple:

> And he shall confirm the covenant with many for one week: and in the midst of the week he shall cause the sacrifice and the oblation to cease, and for the overspreading of abominations he shall make it desolate, even until the consummation, and that determined shall be poured upon the desolate.
> —Daniel 9:27

He desecrates the temple by forbidding them to use it and declaring himself to be God:

> Who opposeth and exalteth himself above all that is called God, or that is worshipped; so that he as God sitteth in the temple of God, shewing himself that he is God.
> —2 Thessalonians 2:4

The Gospel of Matthew quotes Jesus as He referred to the abomination of desolation:

> When ye therefore shall see the abomination of desolation, spoken of by Daniel the prophet, stand in the holy place, (whoso readeth, let him understand.)
>
> —MATTHEW 24:15

Luke also quotes Jesus, and gives us more insight to what will be going on at that time:

> And when ye shall see Jerusalem compassed with armies, then know that the desolation thereof is night.
>
> —LUKE 21:20

This lets us know that Jerusalem will be compassed with armies just prior to the desecration of the temple by the Antichrist. This is when he breaks the covenant with the Jews, after three and a half years (Dan. 9:27). The abomination of desolation is consummated when the Antichrist proclaims that he is God while sitting in the temple of God.

Let us go back to the resurrection and Rapture. We now know that the saints, whose robes of salvation are white and clean; will meet the Lord in the air when He comes. The ungodly Christians, along with the Jews, will be left here on earth during the tribulation. God's Spirit will be put in them, and they will be given a second chance to acknowledge Jesus as their Messiah and Lord. Even so, they must all give their lives for their testimony:

> And when he had opened the fifth seal, I saw under the altar the souls of them that were slain for the word of God, and for the testimony which they held: And they cried with a loud voice, saying, How long, O Lord, holy

and true, dost thou not judge and avenge our blood on them that dwell on the earth? And white robes were given unto every one of them; and it was said unto them, that they should rest yet for a little season, until their fellow servants also and their brethren, that should be killed as they were, should be fulfilled.

—REVELATION 6:9–11

Here we find this same group of people, along with all who will be killed as they were, before the throne of God in heaven. And all are with white robes:

These will include all races, all creeds, and all denominations from around the world; who had spots or wrinkles in their robe of salvation. Along with them will be the whole house of Israel, who had not accepted Jesus as their Messiah during their lifetime. They will be resurrected at the same time, and the Spirit of God put in them (Ezek. 37). And because they did not have the Spirit of God in them when they died, they must all go through or into the time of tribulation to wash their robes white. They will all be "cast into the great winepress of the wrath of God" (Rev. 15:19). John explains well as both of these groups of people will be "reaped" or resurrected:

And I looked, and behold a white cloud, and upon the cloud one sat like unto the Son of man, having on his head a golden crown, and in his hand a sharp sickle. And another angel came out of the temple, crying with a loud voice to him that sat on the cloud, Thrust in thy sickle, and reap: for the time is come for thee to reap; for the harvest of the earth is ripe. And he that sat on the cloud thrust in his sickle on the earth; and the earth was reaped.

—REVELATION 14:14–16

This is the first part of the first resurrection. This is the Son of Man sitting on the cloud. He is waiting for his Father God to give the order that it is time for the earth to be reaped.

> But of that day and hour knoweth no man, no, not the angels of heaven, but my Father only.
>
> —MATTHEW 24:36

Then the earth will be reaped of all who have the Spirit of God in them. All whose robes are white will meet Him in the air, or clouds, at that time. But those who have spots or wrinkles in their robes must go into the tribulation along with the house of Israel. We see their resurrection in the next few verses:

> And another angel came out of the temple which is in heaven, he also having a sharp sickle. And another angel came out from the altar, which had power over fire; and cried with a loud cry to him that had the sharp sickle, saying, Thrust in thy sharp sickle, and gather the clusters of the vine of the earth; for her grapes are fully ripe. And the angel thrust in his sickle into the earth, and gathered the vine of the earth, and cast it into the great winepress of the wrath of God. And the winepress was trodden without the city, and blood came out of the winepress, even unto the horse bridles, by the space of a thousand and six hundred furlongs.
>
> —REVELATION 14:17–20

Here we see two angels, and the second angel has power over fire. This angel gave the order for the "clusters of the vine of the earth" to be reaped. Israel is referred to as a vine in Hosea 10:1:

Israel is an empty vine, he bringeth forth fruit unto himself.

All were cast into the great winepress of the wrath of God. We know that this is the time of great tribulations here on earth when we read that "blood was up to the horse bridles." Ezekiel brings us up to that time to come:

> And, thou son of man, thus saith the Lord God; Speak unto every feathered fowl, and to every beast of the field, Assemble yourselves, and come; gather yourselves on every side to my sacrifice upon the mountains of Israel, that ye may eat flesh, and drink blood. Ye shall eat the flesh of the mighty, and drink the blood of the princes of the earth, of rams, of lambs, and of goats, of bullocks, all of them fatlings of Bashan. And ye shall eat fat till ye be full, and drink blood till ye be drunken, of my sacrifice which I have sacrificed for you. Thus shall ye be filled at my table with horses and chariots, with mighty men, and with all men of war, saith the Lord God. And I will set my glory among the heathen, and all the heathen shall see my judgment that I have executed, and my hand that I have laid upon them. So the house of Israel shall know that I am the Lord their God from that day and forward. And the heathen shall know that the house of Israel went into captivity for their iniquity: because they trespassed against me, therefore hid I my face from them, and gave them into the hand of their enemies: so fell they all by the sword. According to their uncleanness and according to their transgression have I done unto them, and hid my face from them. Therefore thus saith the Lord God; Now will I bring again the captivity of Jacob, and have mercy upon the whole house of Israel, and will be jealous for my holy name; After that they have borne their shame, and all their trespasses whereby they have trespassed against

me, when they dwelt safely in their land, and none made them afraid. When I have brought them again from the people, and gathered them out of their enemies' lands, and am sanctified in them in the sight of many nations; Then shall they know that I am the Lord their God, which caused them to be led into captivity among the heathen: but I have gathered them unto their own land, and have left none of them any more there. Neither will I hide my face any more from them: for I have poured out my Spirit upon the house of Israel, saith the Lord god.

—EZEKIEL 39:17–29

This multitude, which no man could number, will be from all the ages, and from all creeds. They will all be dwelling on the earth at the time of the tribulation, that is to come. They will all ultimately give their life for their testimony, as the Antichrist or false prophet wills. This explains the scriptures that we have all wondered about at one time or another.

After this I beheld, and lo, a great multitude, which no man could number, of all nations, and kindreds, and people, and tongues, stood before the throne, and before the Lamb, clothed with white robes and palms in their hands; And cried with a loud voice, saying, Salvation to our God which sitteth upon the throne, and unto the Lamb. And all the angels stood round about the throne, and about the elders and the four beasts, and fell before the throne on their faces, and worshipped God, Saying, Amen: Blessing, and glory, and wisdom, and thanksgiving, and honour, and power, and might, be unto our God forever and ever. Amen. And one of the elders answered, saying unto me, What are these which are arrayed in white robes? and whence came they? And I said unto, Sir, thou knowest, And he said to me, These are they which came our of great tribulation, and have washed

> their robes, and made them white in the blood of the
> Lamb. Therefore are they before the throne of God, and
> serve him day and night in his temple: and he that sitteth
> on the throne shall dwell among them. They shall hun-
> ger no more, neither thirst any more; neither shall the
> sun light on them, nor any heat. For the Lamb which is
> in the midst of the throne shall feed them, and shall lead
> them unto living fountains of waters: and God shall wipe
> away all tears from their eyes.
>
> —REVELATION 7:9–17

A great multitude, which no man can number, is many people. But when you think about it, this will include all ungodly
Christians, who had spots and blemishes on their robes of salvation from the time of the first church in A.D. 30 to the time
when Jesus will come in the Rapture for His saints. This will
explain how the first can be last and the last can be first.

> And they shall come from the east and from the west, and
> from the north and from the south, and shall sit down in
> the kingdom of God. And, behold, there are last which
> shall be first, and there are first, which shall be last.
>
> —LUKE 13:29–30

Only God Himself would know this fact, and He made
sure that it was told in at least three of the Gospels: Matthew
19:30, Matthew 20:16, Mark 10:30, and Luke 13:30 (which is
quoted above). He knew that the words of prophecy would be
unsealed in the last days, and He wanted us to be aware of this
fact. This is another piece of the puzzle that helps to make it
all come together. God is a loving God and wants each of us
to know all that is coming upon the world so that we might be
prepared, in order to avoid the tribulations that are to come
upon the earth.

How many of us have little things in our lives that should not be there? Is there anything else that we need to do to be ready to meet Him? Should He come for us in the Rapture, or by death? Almighty God is a loving God and wants all of us to make it in the Rapture. But He is also a just God. He wants only children who truly love Him and are serious about wanting to spend eternity with Him.

> That if thou shalt confess with thy mouth the Lord Jesus, and shalt believe in thine heart that God hath raised him from the dead, thou shalt be saved. For with the heart man believeth unto righteousness; and with the mouth confession is made unto salvation.
>
> —ROMANS 10:9–10

Of course, we want to spend eternity with our Lord. We want to be ready to go with Him when He comes in the clouds because when that door is shut, the resurrection has occurred: all those who were ready, whose robes of salvation are white and clean, will meet the Lord in the air. All who have blemishes or spots on their garments of salvation will be left here on earth to wash their robes white by the trials and testing that are to come upon all who dwell on the earth. They must overcome all that is to come upon them, to wash their robes white and ultimately give their lives for their testimony just as our Lord had to give His life:

> To him that overcometh will I grant to sit with me in my throne, even as I also overcame, and am set down with my Father in his throne.
>
> —REVELATION 3:21

If they will overcome by standing true to Him and their testimony, even to the death, just as our Lord overcame with death, they will sit with Him on His throne with our Father God. This will be the second death for all the ungodly saints who had died and were resurrected in the first resurrection. They were left here on earth in their new bodies, to be tried and tested in the tribulations that are to come to all who dwell on the earth. They must wash their robes of salvation white and clean and give their lives for their testimony. This will be the second death for them. But this second death will have no power over them. They must not fear this second death but be prepared to give their life for their testimony. That is the only way that they can overcome: by giving their lives for their testimony:

> Blessed and holy is he that hath part in the first resurrection: on such the second death hath no power, but they shall be priests of God and of Christ, and shall reign with him a thousand years.
>
> —Revelation 20:6

The Antichrist or beast will have power over all who dwell on the earth at that time, after the Rapture. And all whose names are not written in the Book of Life will worship him. He will require everyone to receive a mark on their forehead or on their hand; or they cannot buy or sell. All who take this mark of the beast or Antichrist will damn their souls to an eternity in hell. Those who are willing to give their lives for their testimony for Jesus Christ will spend eternity with our Lord and Savior, Jesus Christ. Here are the scriptures:

> And it was given unto him to make war with the saints, and to overcome them: and power was given him over all kindreds, and tongues, and nations. And all that dwell upon the earth shall worship him, whose names are not written in the book of life of the Lamb slain from

the foundation of the world. If any man have an ear, let him hear.

—REVELATION 13:7–9

And he causeth all, both small and great, rich and poor, free and bond, to receive a mark in their right hand, or in their foreheads: And that no man might buy or sell, save he that had the mark, or the name of the beast, or the number of his name.

—REVELATION 13:16–17

For all who overcome the Antichrist and give up their life for their testimony, this is what they can expect.

And I saw thrones, and they that sat upon them, and judgment was given into them: and I saw the souls of them that were beheaded for the witness of Jesus, and for the word of God, and which had not worshipped the beast, neither his image, neither had received his mark upon their foreheads, or in their hands; and they lived and reigned with Christ a thousand years.

—REVELATION 20:4

You can believe this would be only the beginning of an eternity with our Lord and Savior. Just remember to work while it is day, for the night will come when no man can work. (See John 9:4.) The door is still open and will be until our Lord's return. Use the time wisely. No one knows the day nor the hour that He will return (Matt. 24:36). There will be more on the door in a later chapter.

*Chapter 6*

# THE SINNERS WHO
# WILL BE LEFT BEHIND

THE DOOR HAS been shut for the Gentiles. Where does that leave the Gentile sinners who are alive here on the earth when the resurrection and the Rapture occur? That was the door of salvation that was closed. If you had never accepted the Lord as your Savior, you are considered to be a sinner, and the saving power of the Spirit of God is not in you. And as a sinner, when Jesus comes and the door is shut, you will be damned to an eternity in hell, no exceptions. There are those who have taught that one can be saved during the tribulation period, but that fact is not in the Bible. Nowhere in God's Word can those words be backed up with scripture. When Joel 2:32 is used, it is taken out of context. That scripture is strictly for the Jews, who are in the seventieth week of tribulations. That is the only way that they will be saved, to call upon the Lord and acknowledge Him as Savior.

Back to the Gentile sinners who are alive when the first resurrection occurs: you will not be able to overcome without the Spirit of God. In fact, you will not want to. A delusion will be put upon you, and you will believe the lies of the Antichrist and be damned to an eternity in hell with Satan and all of his followers. Paul's letter explains it well:

> And with all deceivableness of unrighteousness in them that perish; because they received not the love of the truth, that they may be saved. And for this cause God shall send them strong delusion, that they should believe a lie: That they all might be damned who believe not the truth, but had pleasure in unrighteousness.
>
> —2 THESSALONIANS 2:10–12

God's will is that none should perish and that all should come to repentance and accept Him as Lord and Savior of their lives. Paul's words in that scripture cannot be any more direct. He is speaking to those who will perish because they have been deceived. When they had the chance to accept the Lord as their Savior, they rejected that chance to be saved. Maybe they think that they can be saved anytime, but not so: if you are alive here on earth when Jesus comes in the clouds to take the saints home, and you are not saved, you are doomed. The door will have been closed when the Rapture occurs.

You will not have another chance. You will have missed your last chance to receive Him as Lord. You will then be here on earth for the seven-year tribulation period. You will believe the lies of the Antichrist and be damned to an eternity in hell. If you have never accepted the Lord as Savior of your soul, do it now. Ask the Lord to forgive you of your sins. Believe in the Lord Jesus Christ, that He died for your sins on the cross, was resurrected, and now sits at the right hand of God the Father, making intersession for us. Ask Him to come into your heart and be Lord of your life, and you will serve Him and love Him. God's will is that none should perish but that all should come to repentance and be saved. (See Romans 3:10, 23; 6:23; 10:9–10.) He wants you so much that He promised that the gospel of the kingdom of God would be preached in all the world unto all nations before the end would come. All, including you, will have heard the gospel sometime during your lifetime or before the Rapture. All will have had at least one chance to accept Jesus as their Lord or to reject Him:

> And this gospel of the kingdom shall be preached in all the world for a witness unto all nations; and then shall the end come.
> —MATTHEW 24:14

God made all of us free moral agents. We will choose our destiny for eternity by accepting Him or rejecting Him. All of us are made in the image of God; He loves each one of us and wants us to choose to be a child of God and have eternal life. But the choice belongs to each of us, and whatever it might be, God will honor your decision.

He will still love you and will hear your prayer of repentance as long as you live or until the Rapture occurs, whatever comes first. After that, it will be too late for you. (See 2 Thessalonians 2:10–12.) You will believe the lies of the Antichrist and be damned for eternity. And if you die as a sinner, or have not accepted Him as Lord when the Rapture occurs, you will be damned. If you had died as a sinner, you will not be resurrected until Judgment Day. You will be judged out of the Lamb's Book of Life to give account for all that you have done in your lifetime.

If you had chosen to be saved, all sins would have gone into the Sea of Forgetfulness, never to be brought up again. The greatest miracle ever is salvation, when you are passed from death unto life everlasting. If your robe of salvation is not white and clean when the Rapture occurs, you will have a second chance to make it white in the tribulations. Only those whose names are written in the Lamb's Book of Life will have that second chance. Revelation 13 describes the Antichrist and false prophet and how they come to power. You can see his anger here because he was unable to prevent the saints from meeting the Lord in the air and going on to heaven, so he blasphemed them. Then all that he could do was to make war with the saints who were left behind. He will have power over them and will kill them. They must be willing to die for their testimony, just as Jesus died for His testimony. Those who are left here on earth will include all sinners who are alive at the time of the Rapture, as well as the saints who must wash their robes of salvation white by trials and testing in the tribulations that are to come to all who dwell on the earth.

This will not be so for the Gentile sinners who are alive here on earth at the time. (See 2 Thessalonians 2:7–9.) The door was closed when the first resurrection occurred, and God's convicting Spirit was taken out of the way. Their names were never written in the Lamb's Book of Life while the door was open; for them there is no other chance. They will believe the lies of the Antichrist and be damned:

> And all that dwell upon the earth shall worship him, whose names are not written in the book of life of the Lamb slain from the foundation of the world. If any man have an ear, let him hear.
>
> —Revelation 13:8–9

We do hear, and we do understand that God's Word is true and will not contradict itself. Instead, it is similar to a giant jigsaw puzzle. Every word goes into its place to make the big picture that God intended for us to see. There is a partial scripture being preached to the Gentiles that some use to say that you can be saved during the tribulation. But this passage, from Joel 2:32, is being taken out of context. This message is absolutely for the Jewish people. From the very first verse of Joel 2, it says, "Blow ye the trumpet in Zion, and sound an alarm in my holy mountain: let all the inhabitants of the land tremble: for the day of the LORD cometh, for it is night at hand." This is obviously a message for those who are in Zion and the holy mountain. And the message is that the day of the Lord is at hand. It is a warning for the Jewish people of the things that are to come to pass. Let us drop down to the verses just preceding this one that is used to say the Gentiles can be saved in the tribulations:

> And ye shall know that I am in the midst of Israel, and that I am the LORD your God, and none else: and my people shall never be ashamed. And it shall come to pass afterward, that I will pour out my spirit upon all flesh; and your sons and your daughters shall prophesy, your old men shall dream dreams, your young men shall see visions: And also upon the servants and the handmaids in those days will I pour out my spirit. And I will show wonders in the heavens and in the earth, blood, and fire, and pillars of smoke. The sun shall be turned into darkness, and the moon into blood, before the great and the terrible day of the LORD come.
>
> —JOEL 2:27–31

All of us recognize these words as a prophecy of the things that will be happening during the tribulation period and the things that the Lord will do for them. This is a warning, as well as reassurance from Him, that He will have everything under control. Now let us go to verse 32 and read all of it:

> And it shall come to pass, that whosoever shall call on the name of the LORD shall be delivered: for in mount Zion and in Jerusalem shall be deliverance, as the LORD hath said, and in the remnant whom the LORD shall call.
>
> —JOEL 2:32

The first two lines of that scripture are all that is ever used to prove their point, but the third line plainly tells us that this is for those who are in Zion and Jerusalem. The Lord said it. The whole house of Israel will be resurrected; God's Spirit will be put in them, and all will return to their own land to be tried and tested in the great tribulations that are to come upon all who dwell on the earth.

The Lord promises them that He will pour out His Spirit upon them, and they will see wonders in the heavens and on the earth. There will be deliverance for all of the house of Israel who call upon the name of the Lord. Paul tells us in Acts that Peter believed that the outpouring of the Holy Spirit on the Day of Pentecost was what Joel was talking about. And this was in A.D. 33:

> But Peter, standing up with the eleven, lifted up his voice, and said unto them, Ye men of Judea, and all ye that dwell in Jerusalem, be this known unto you, and hearken to my words: For these are not drunken, as ye suppose, seeing it is but the third hour of the day. But this is that which was spoken by the prophet Joel.
>
> —ACTS 2:14–16

When the outpouring of God's Holy Spirit came on the Day of Pentecost (Acts 2:1–4), this was the fulfillment of the promise that Jesus had made to us; and was recorded in John's gospel:

> And I will pray the Father, and he shall give you another Comforter, that he may abide with you forever; Even the Spirit of truth; whom the world cannot receive, because it seeth him not, neither knoweth him: but ye know him; for he dwelleth with you, and shall be in you. I will not leave you comfortless: I will come to you.

God has sent His Holy Spirit to empower us; for the work that He has for each of us to accomplish. We must pray for the leading of God's Holy Spirit in all that we do or say. He is our Comforter and our guide.

*Chapter 7*

# THE
# UNPARDONABLE SIN

THERE IS ANOTHER group of people who will have no chance to be in the Rapture, nor a second chance to wash their robes white. These are the ones who have committed the unpardonable sin. There is no repentance for them. They will stand in their lot with the sinners. Let us study God's Word together to first see what it is:

> And whosoever shall speak a word against the Son of man, it shall be forgiven him: but unto him that blasphemeth against the Holy Ghost it shall not be forgiven.
> —LUKE 12:10

First of all, we can see that the unpardonable sin is to blaspheme the Holy Ghost. Then we must consider what it means to blaspheme the Holy Ghost. Our first thought is that it must be to ridicule or make fun of the Holy Ghost or Holy Spirit. And I believe that would be right. We are cautioned that we must not grieve the Holy Spirit of God (Eph. 4:30).

Paul is speaking to all who have the Holy Spirit of God living in them. We know there are two types of Christians, the righteous and the ungodly (1 Pet. 4:18). Now let us go back to the salvation experience and come forward to see *who* can commit the unpardonable sin.

> For God so loved the world that He gave his only begotten Son that whosoever believeth in him should not perish, but have everlasting life.
>
> —JOHN 3:16

This is God's plan of salvation: believe, repent, and receive Him as Lord of your life. But that was not all. There was more, and Luke quoted John:

> John answered, saying unto them all, I indeed baptize you with water; but one mightier than I cometh, the latchet of whose shoes I am not worthy to unloose: he shall baptize you with the Holy Ghost and with fire.
>
> —LUKE 3:16

To receive the gift of the Holy Ghost with fire, you must ask the Father for it specifically. Luke tells us of this heavenly gift that our heavenly Father will give to us, if we only ask and believe:

> If ye then, being evil, know how to give good gifts unto your children: how much more shall your heavenly Father give the Holy Spirit to them that ask him?
>
> —LUKE 11:13

These are Jesus' own words, quoted by Luke. And with the Holy Spirit, come the spiritual gifts. See 1 Corinthians 12 for a complete explanation from Paul the Apostle. The gifts are from God and to be cherished and used for His glory. This is God's plan to bring us closer to Him and to receive from Him these wonderful gifts. How much more He can give to us than we could ever give to our children. Even though these gifts are freely given to those who ask in faith, believing, there are those who have turned back or fallen away. They had asked and received His Holy Spirit with the spiritual gifts as God wills. Those heavenly gifts are coveted with the saints and then there are those who have turned back. It is hard to believe that anyone would ever turn back into sin after tasting the heavenly gifts of God, but it does happen. Peter warns us of the consequences:

> For if after they have escaped the pollutions of the world through the knowledge of the Lord and Saviour Jesus Christ, they are again entangled therein, and overcome, the latter end is worse with them than the beginning. For it had been better for them not to have known the way of righteousness, than, after they have known it, to turn from the holy commandment delivered unto them.
>
> —2 PETER 2:20–21

Now you are beginning to get the picture. You cannot blaspheme the Holy Ghost unless you have tasted the Holy Ghost. Paul's explanation is in Hebrews:

> For it is impossible for those who were once enlightened, and have tasted of the heavenly gift, and were made partakers of the Holy Ghost, And have tasted the good word of God, and the powers of the world to

come, If they shall fall away, to renew them again unto repentance; seeing they crucify to themselves the Son of God afresh, and put him to an open shame.

—Hebrews 6:4–6

This indeed is the unpardonable sin. Once you have tasted of the heavenly gifts of God, given by the Holy Spirit who is alive within us, and have fallen back into sin, there can be no more repentance. This fact is emphasized again in a later scripture in Hebrews by Paul:

For if we sin willfully after that we have received the knowledge of the truth, there remaineth no more sacrifice for sins. But a certain fearful looking for of judgment and fiery indignation, which shall devour the adversaries.

—Hebrews 10:26–27

God's Word makes it plain that it is impossible to renew them again with repentance once they have tasted of the heavenly gifts sent from God above, and then they turned back, or fell away. With this deed, God's Holy Spirit is grieved and will be forever withdrawn from those who have committed the unpardonable sin. They will indeed be counted with the sinners.

We are reminded of what Peter said: "For if after they have escaped the pollutions of the world through the knowledge of the Lord and Savior Jesus Christ, they are again entangled therein, and overcome, the latter end is worse with them than the beginning. For it would have been better for them not to have known the way of righteousness, than, after they have known it, to turn from the holy commandment delivered unto them" (2 Peter 2:20–21). This tells us that once they are committed to damnation with Satan, things will be much worse for them because they had once known the better way while here on earth, tasted of God's wonderful gifts, and then turned back

76

into sin. It is impossible to renew them again unto repentance, for they put our Lord to open shame.

They who have committed the unpardonable sin will indeed be counted among the sinners and not entitled to a second chance. They will, if they are still alive when Jesus comes to take His saints away in the clouds, be left here on earth to go through the tribulations. The difference will be that they will not have the Spirit of God in them and will believe the lies of the Antichrist and be damned. All others and sinners who had died before the Rapture will not be resurrected until after the thousand-year reign to be judged according to their works.

> But the rest of the dead lived not again until the thousand years were finished.
>
> —REVELATION 20:5

> And I saw a great white throne, and him that sat on it, from whose face the earth and the heaven fled away; and there was found no place for them. And I saw the dead, small and great, stand before God; and the books were opened: and another book was opened, which is the book of life: and the dead were judged out of those things which were written in the books, according to their works. And the sea gave up the dead which were in it; and death and hell delivered up the dead which were in them: and they were judged every man according to their works. And death and hell were cast into the lake of fire. This is the second death. And whosoever was not found written in the book of life was cast into the lake of fire.
>
> —REVELATION 20:11–15

This depicts the second resurrection, the resurrection of all sinners to be judged by their works while here on earth and cast into the lake of fire. This is their second death, of which the consequences are not good. We are reminded of John's words, when he told us of the two resurrections:

> Verily, verily, I say unto you, The hour is coming, and now is, when the dead shall hear the voice of the Son of God: And they that hear shall not live.
>
> —JOHN 5:25

> For as the Father has life in himself; so hath he given to the Son to have life in himself; And hath given him authority to execute judgment also, because he is the Son of man.
>
> —JOHN 5:26–27

> Marvel not at this: for the hour is coming, in the which all that are in the graves shall hear his voice, And shall come forth; they that have done good, unto the resurrection of life; and they that have done evil, unto the resurrection of damnation.
>
> —JOHN 5:28–29

John is quoting Jesus' own words in these scriptures; they depict both the first and second resurrections. All will hear His voice and come forth at either the first or second resurrection. Remember, "Blessed and holy is he that hath part in the first resurrection: on such the second death hath no power" (Rev. 20:6). But not so with those in the second resurrection. Their second death is to be cast alive into the lake of fire, to spend eternity. God has done all that He can do that we might escape spending eternity in a lake of fire and brimstone and to be tormented day and night forever and ever. (See Revelation 20:10.) The choice is ours. It is up to each of us to make that decision before it is too late. The door is still open. Believe, repent, and receive. It is just that simple. There is nothing complicated about it; just believe on the Lord Jesus Christ, and you shall be saved. If you fall, be quick to repent and ask for forgiveness as well as the strength to walk the path that leads to life everlasting. But to sin willfully, after receiving God's heavenly gifts, is truly the unpardonable sin.

> For if we sin wilfully after that we have received the knowledge of the truth, there remained no more sacrifice for sins, But a certain fearful looking for of judgment and fiery indignation, which shall devour the adversaries.
>
> —HEBREWS 10:26–27

# Chapter 8

# THE CHURCH THAT
# WILL MISS THE RAPTURE

I WILL BEGIN THIS chapter with the definition of *revelation*, as given in God's Holy Word. This is what the Book of Revelation calls itself: a revealing, unveiling, explaining, making known, of things to come.

> The Revelation of Jesus Christ, which God gave unto him, to shew unto his servants things which must shortly come to pass; and he sent and signified it by his angel unto his servant John: Who bare record of the word of God, and of the testimony of Jesus Christ, and of all things that he saw. Write the things which thou hast seen, and the things which are, and the things which shall be hereafter. After this I looked, and, behold, a door was opened in heaven: and the first voice that I heard was as it were of a trumpet talking with me; which

said, Come up hither, and I will show thee things which
must be hereafter.

—REVELATION 1:12, 19; 4:1

Thus in its first words, the book is avowedly predictive.
That is what it was written for: to unfold the future, to chart
the course and destiny of the church. This is a book of undi-
luted optimism for God's people, assuring us again and again
that we are under God's protection, with, come what may,
a life of everlasting blessedness ahead.[1] John had been ban-
ished to the Isle of Patmos. This, according to apostolic tradition, was in the persecution of Domitian, about A.D. 95. The
next year, A.D. 96, John was released, and permitted to return
to Ephesus:[2]

> I John, who also am your brother, and companion in
> tribulation, and in the kingdom and patience of Jesus
> Christ, was in the Isle that is called Patmos, for the word
> of God, and for the testimony of Jesus Christ.
>
> —REVELATION 1:9

The use of the past tense, *was* in Patmos, seems to indicate
that, while he saw the visions in Patmos, it was after his release
and return to Ephesus that he wrote the Book of Revelation,
about A.D. 96.[3]

Much emphasis was placed on seven particular churches of
Asia in the first chapter of Revelation:

> I was in the Spirit on the Lord's day, and heard behind
> me a great voice, as of a trumpet, saying, I am Alpha and
> Omega, the first and the last: and, What thou seest, write
> in a book, and send it unto the Seven Churches which
> are in Asia; unto Ephesus, and unto Smyrna, and unto

Pergamos, and unto Thyatira, and unto Sardis, and unto
Philadelphia, and unto Laodicea.

—REVELATION 1:10–11

We ask ourselves why God chose these seven churches out of
hundreds that were located in cities all over the world. Remember, John was given this vision in A.D. 95. Historical interpretation is that the book was designed to forecast a general view
of the whole period of church history, from John's time on to
the end of the world: a sort of panorama, a series of pictures,
delineating the successive steps and outstanding features of the
church's struggle to final victory: "A Vision of the Ages"; "Pictures of the Great Epochs and Crises of the Church."[4]

This is what I believe, along with many Bible scholars.
Many of the things that happened in these churches parallel
the things that have happened during the past Church Ages,
and up to the present Church Age. I believe God chose these
churches because He knew that they would reflect the seven
Church Ages that were to come. Therefore, from henceforth,
this portion of this book will reflect this belief. And the dates
that are given, of course, are approximate.

We begin with the Church Age of Ephesus; which would
have begun on the Day of Pentecost, in A.D. 33. After Peter
preached, on the Day of Pentecost (Acts 2:14–41), three thousand souls received his words and were baptized. And more
were added daily (Acts 2:47). The church flourished, as the
disciples spread the gospel. Paul had done some of his greatest works in Ephesus, from A.D. 54 to A.D. 57. And within fifty
years afterward, Christians had become so numerous in Ephesus that the heathen temples were almost forsaken. Ephesus
became the center of Christendom.[5]

"In A.D. 64 Nero burned Rome, and fiddled in glee at the
sight of it. He was a builder, and in order to build a new and

grander Rome, he had to set fire to the city. He blamed the fire on the Christians, and ordered punishment. Multitudes were arrested and put to death in the most cruel ways. Some were crucified; others were tied in skins of animals, and thrown into the arena, to be worried to death by dogs."[6]

This was for the entertainment of the people. Some were thrown to wild beasts, while others were tied to stakes in Nero's gardens, pitch poured over their bodies, and lit as torches; to light Nero's gardens at night, while he drove around in his chariot, naked, indulging himself in his midnight revels. He gloated over the dying agonies of his victims.

It was in the wake of these persecutions that Paul was rearrested in Greece or Asia Minor, possibly at Troas (2 Tim. 4:13) and brought back to Rome; this time, by agents of Rome, as a criminal. (2 Tim. 2:9).[7] For all we know, this may have been in connection with the burning of Rome. Paul was the world leader of the people who were being punished for that crime. And Paul had been in Rome for two years, just preceding the fire. It would have been easy to lay this crime at Paul's door. But whether that was the charge, we do not know. Paul, at any rate, was indicted, and he knew there was no hope for escape. Alexander, the coppersmith, journeyed all the way from Ephesus to Rome, to testify against Paul, which he did with considerable success (2 Tim. 4:14).[8] Paul wrote his last epistle, or letter, to Timothy (2 Tim.). Paul was to be executed for a crime of which he was not guilty. His friends had forsaken him, leaving him to suffer alone; the cause for which he was giving his life being blotted out in the West by persecution, and in the East, going into apostasy. Yet, there was no hint of regret, no hint of doubt, but that the church, though now apparently being defeated, would eventually be triumphant. And no hint of doubt but that the moment his head would be cut from his body, he would go straight to the arms of Him whom he had loved and served so devotedly. This epistle is the exultant cry of a dying conqueror.[9] Paul was martyred about A.D. 66 or 67. Paul had warned the Ephesians to beware of false teachers:

> For I know this, that after my departing shall grievous wolves enter in among you, not sparing the flock. Also of your own selves shall men arise, speaking perverse things, to draw away disciples after them. Therefore watch, and remember, that by the space of three years I ceased not to warn every one night and day with tears.
>
> —ACTS 20:29–31

It had been sixty-six years since Pentecost, the birthday of the church, at Jerusalem. The church everywhere had made phenomenal growth, but signs of corruption were beginning to appear. Their zeal for Christ was cooling off. They no longer loved Him as they once did. This hurt Christ, and for it they received a stinging rebuke and were warned to repent or else their "candlestick would be removed"; and it has, the site of Ephesus is deserted.[10]

> Nevertheless I have somewhat against thee, because thou hast left thy first love. Remember therefore from whence thou art fallen, and repent, and do the first works; or else I will come unto thee quickly, and will remove thy candlestick out of his place, except thou repent.
>
> —REVELATION 2:4–5

Our Lord was crucified. They were sure that would put an end to Christianity, but not so; the church continued to grow. It was obvious that the more the church was attacked the stronger and greater it became. God reminded them to be faithful unto death, and He would give them a crown of life.

> And unto the angel of the church in Smyrna write; These things saith the first and the last, which was dead, and is alive; I know thy works, and tribulation, and poverty, (but thou art rich) and I know the blasphemy of them which say they are Jews, and are not, but are the synagogue of Satan. Fear none of those things which thou shalt suffer: behold, the devil shall cast some of you into prison, that ye may be tried; and ye shall have tribulation ten days; be thou faithful unto death, and I will give thee a crown of life. He that hath an ear, let him hear what the Spirit saith unto the churches; He that overcometh shall not be hurt of the second death.
>
> —REVELATION 2:8–11

There was an all-out attack made upon the Church Age of Smyrna. This Church Age was approximately from A.D. 100 to 305. During this time, there were ten different Roman emperors. All of them persecuted the Christians; some were worse than others. The last of the ten, and considered to be the worst of all, was Diocletian. He ruled as Emperor from A.D. 284 to A.D. 305. The last ten years of the rule of Diocletian were considered to be the worst for the early Christians. Many historians and Bible scholars believe that the reference of ten in Revelation 2:10 pertains to that period of history.[11] And in A.D. 303 Diocletian issued three edicts, in rapid succession, each more severe than its predecessor. Christian churches were to be destroyed; all copies of the Bible were to be burned; all Christians were to be deprived of public office and civil rights; and at last, all without exception, were to sacrifice to the gods upon pain of death. Maximin, his nephew and ruler of Italy and Africa, under Diocletian, had issued the fourth edict. All the pains, which iron and steel, fire and sword, rack and cross, wild beasts and beastly men could inflict, were employed to gain the useless end.[12] The number of martyrs cannot be estimated with any degree of certainty, but there were many.[13] By this time, with all the persecutions of the Christians, many had chosen the earthly life over the heavenly life. This is evident when we read the history of Pergamos. We can see how Satan had entrenched himself into their society.[14]

Pergamum (Pergamos) was a seat of emperor worship, where incense was offered before the statue of the emperor, as to God. Refusal of Christians to do this often meant death. Also, there was an altar to Jupiter and the temple of Esculapius, a healing god, worshiped in the form of a serpent, one of the names of Satan. Beside these, it was also a stronghold of Balaamite and Nicolaitan teachers. Thus, as a notorious center of heathenism and wickedness, it was called "Satan's Throne." Devotees of heathen practices who had infiltrated the ranks of Christians and were nicknamed Balaam, advised them to participate in the sexual vices of heathen worship. Evidently, they had quite a following.[15]

This was the literal early church at Pergamos. You can see that they had tolerated the false teaching and those who did it. They also allowed the worship of idols and false gods. The false teaching was the right of Christians to indulge in heathen immoralities. We can see why God called this church "Satan's Seat."

> I know thy works, and where thou dwellest, even where Satan's seat is: and thou holdest fast my name, and hast not denied my faith, even in those days wherein Antipas was my faithful martyr, who was slain among you, where Satan dwelleth.
>
> —Revelation 2:13

With all of these facts before us, I sincerely believe that the early church of Pergamos represents the Church Age of approximately A.D. 306 to A.D. 606. Constantine was named as Emperor of Gaul, Spain, and Britain in A.D. 306, following Diocletian.[16] But persecutions still raged in the East under the rule of Galerius, Diocletian's co-regent and son-in-law, and his nephew, Maximin Daza. Galerius was a cruel and fanatic heathen.[17] Galerius, in A.D. 308, issued a fifth edict of persecution, which commanded that all males with their wives and servants, and even their children, should sacrifice and actually taste the accursed offerings, and that all provisions in the markets should be sprinkled with sacrificial wine. This monstrous law introduced a reign of terror for two years and left the Christians no alternative but apostasy or starvation. Eusebius was a witness of this persecution in Caesarea, Tyre, and Egypt; and saw the houses of prayer razed to the ground, the Holy Scriptures committed to the flames on the market places, the pastors hunted, tortured, and torn to pieces in the amphitheater.[18] But as the persecutions raged, the zeal and the fidelity of the Christians increased, and martyrdom spread as contagion. This persecution lasted eight years in this region.

Diocletian destroyed himself in A.D. 313.[19] Galerius, the real author of the persecutions, brought to reflection by a terrible disease put an end to the slaughter shortly before his death by a remarkable Edict of Toleration. This he issued from Nicomedia in A.D. 311, in connection with Constantine and Licinius. In that document he declared that the purpose of reclaiming the Christians from this willful innovation and the multitude of their sects to the laws and discipline of the Roman State, was not accomplished; and that he would now grant them permission to hold their religious assemblies, provided that they disturbed not the order of the state. To this he added in conclusion the significant instruction that the Christians, "after this manifestation of grace, Should pray to their God for the welfare of the Emperors of the state, and of themselves, that the state might prosper in every respect, and that they might live quietly in their homes."[20] This edict virtually closes the period of persecution in the Roman Empire. For a short time Maximin continued in every way to oppress and vex the church in the East. And the cruel pagan, Maxentius, son-in-law of Galerius, did the same in Italy. But the young Constantine, who hailed from the far West, had already in A.D. 306 become Emperor of Gaul, Spain, and Britain.[21] And in 312, Constantine boldly led his troops into Italy and defeated Maxentius in three battles. Before the last battle at the Milvian Bridge in Rome, Constantine is said to have had a vision of the Christian cross with the legend in Greek, "By this sign thou shalt conquer." According to the story, in 313 at Milan, Constantine adopted the Christian religion and decreed that Christianity be the lawful religion throughout the empire. An inscription on the Arch of Constantine (315) in Rome attributed his victory over Maxentius to an impulse of divinity. Constantine had become sole emperor in the West, and Licinius, having defeated Maximinus in 313 in Asia Minor, was sole emperor in the East. Licinius soon chose to fight Constantine for complete control of the empire, but was defeated in 314. Licinius concluded a peace, ceding the eastern provinces of Illyricum, Macedonia, Moesia, Pannonia, and Greece to Constantine. For the next nine years Constantine devoted himself to correcting abuses in the administration of the laws, to strengthening the frontiers, and to chastising the barbarians. In 323 war was renewed with Licinius, who in 324 was defeated at the ancient city of Byzantium and put to death. Constantine was now sole ruler of the Roman

Empire, of which the city of Rome was no longer the political or geographical center. Constantine, having rebuilt Byzantine in 324, moved the imperial capitol to Byzantium, which he dedicated in 330 as the city of Constantine, or Constantinople, now Istanbul. From his new capitol, he ruled until his death in A.D. 337. The reign of Constantine is generally regarded as enlightened and tolerant. Christianity began to flourish and became the religion of the rulers themselves. Constantine also retained the traditional pagan title of Pontifex Maximus; and his coins still bore the figures and the names of the old gods. He did not receive baptism until shortly before his death.[22] Constantine had given the Christians freedom to worship God; and also, "permission was given to any others who may wish to follow their own observance or form of worship"—a privilege obviously consonant with the tranquility of our own times—so that every man may have permission to choose and practice whatever religion he wishes. "This we have done to make it plain that we are not belittling any rite or form of worship." This was stated in the Copy of Imperial Ordinances.[23] Constantine favored the Christian religion. He demanded restoration in full for all of the properties that had been seized from them. He encouraged and helped in building churches. He made Christianity the religion of his Court. He issued a general exhortation in 325 to all his subjects to embrace Christianity. And because the Roman Aristocracy persisted in adhering to their pagan religions, Constantine moved his Capitol to Constantinople.[24] He made the Christian's day of assembly, Sunday, a rest day, forbidding ordinary work and permitting Christian soldiers to attend church services. This rest for one day a week meant much for slaves.

Now let us move ahead to Emperor Theodosius, A.D. 378 to 398. He made Christianity the state religion of the Roman

Empire, and made church membership compulsory. This was the worst calamity that has ever befallen the church. This "forced conversion" filled the churches with unregenerate people.[25] Not only so, Theodosius undertook the forcible suppression of all other religions and prohibited idol worship. Under his decree, heathen temples were torn down by mobs of Christians, and there was much bloodshed. Christ had designed to conquer by purely spiritual and moral means. Up to this time conversion was voluntary, a genuine change in the heart and life. But now the military spirit of Imperial Rome had entered the church. The church had conquered the Roman Empire, but in reality the Roman Empire had conquered the church by making the church into the image of the Roman Empire. The church had changed its nature and had entered into its great apostasy. It had become a political organization in the spirit and pattern of Imperial Rome. The church took its nose-dive into the millenium of papal abominations. The imperial church of the fourth and fifth centuries had become an entirely different institution from the persecuted church of the first three centuries. In its ambition to rule, it lost and forgot the Spirit of Christ. Worship at first was very simple, but was developed into elaborate, stately, imposing ceremonies having all the outward splendor that had belonged to heathen temples.[26] Ministers became "priests." The term *priest* was borrowed from the Jewish system, and from the example of "heathen priesthood." Leo I (440–61) prohibited priests from marrying, and celibacy of priests became a law of the Roman Church. The Goths, Vandals, and Huns, who overthrew the Roman Empire, accepted Christianity. But to a large extent, their conversion was nominal, and this further filled the church with pagan practices.[27] Christianity began its process of amalgamation with Greek and Oriental philosophies, and there arose many sects. From the second to the sixth centuries, the church was rent with controversies over similar isms, and almost lost sight of its true mission.

With this, we see the church sinking into its darkest ages. And in the midst of it all were those whom God had referred to as the Nicolaitanes that he hated (Rev. 2:6, 15). They claimed as their founder, Nicolas, a proselyte of Antioch and one of the seven deacons of the congregation of Jerusalem (Acts 6:5). He is supposed to have apostatized from the true faith and taught the dangerous principle that the flesh must be abused; that is, at least as understood by his disciples, one must make the whole round of sensuality to become its perfect master. But the views of the Fathers are conflicting. Irenaeus, who is followed substantially by Hippolytus, gives a very unfavorable account.

"The Nicolaitanes," he says, are the followers of that Nicolas who was one of the seven first ordained to the diaconate by the apostles. They led lives of unrestrained indulgence. The character of these men is very plainly pointed out in the Apocalypse of John, where they are represented as teaching that it is a matter of indifference to practice adultery and to eat things sacrificed to idols. Wherefore the Word has also spoken of them thus: "But this thou hast, that thou hatest the deeds of the Nicolaitanes, which I also hate" (Rev. 2:6). Either way, many of those in the early church, and the Church Age, representative of that church; had been led into apostasy. This included idol worship, immorality, corruption, and bloodshed.[29] The darkest period of the papacy was from 870–1050. It is called by historians The Midnight of the Dark Ages. Bribery, corruption, immorality, and bloodshed make it just about the blackest chapter in the whole history of the church. Benedict VIII (1012–1024) bought the office of pope with open bribery. This was called *simony*, which is the purchase or sale of church office with money. This simony continued with the papacy until Clement II (1046–1047) was appointed pope by Emperor Henry III of Germany because "no Roman clergyman could be found who was free of the pollution of simony and fornication."[30]

By this time, the church owned a large share of all property and had rich incomes. Then came the most powerful of all the popes, Innocent III (1198–1216).[31] He claimed to be "Vicar of Christ, Vicar of God, Supreme Sovereign Over the Church and the World." He claimed the right to depose kings and princes, and that "all things on earth and in heaven and in hell are subject to the Vicar of Christ." He brought the church into supreme control of the state. Practically all of the monarchs of Europe obeyed his will. Never in history has any one man exerted more power. He ordered two crusades, decreed transubstantiation, confirmed auricular confession, and declared that Peter's successor "can never in any way depart from the Catholic faith," and papal infallibility. He believed that Peter was the first pope, but history disproves it.[32]

The Roman Catholic tradition that Peter was the first pope is fiction, pure and simple. There is no New Testament hint and no historical evidence whatever that Peter was at any time Bishop of Rome. Nor did he ever claim for himself such authority as the popes have claimed for themselves. It seems that Peter had a divine foreboding that his "successors" would be mainly concerned with "lording it over God's flock, rather than showing themselves examples to the flock" (1 Pet. 5:3).

Innocent III condemned the Magna Carta, forbade the reading of the Bible in vernacular, ordered the extermination of heretics, instituted the Inquisition, and ordered the massacre of the Albigenses.[34] More blood was shed under his direction and that of his immediate successors than in any other period of church history, except in the papacy's effort to crush the Reformation in the sixteenth and seventeenth centuries. This also includes the Church Age of Thyatira in the approximate time of A.D. 606 to the 1200's.

Even though this church was still in the Dark Ages, there were those who still walked with God. This age brought about the first pope, the kissing of the pope's feet, holy water, canonization of dead saints, prayer beads, and the forbidding of the Bible to laymen. The infallibility of the pope was initiated. This church allowed a Jezebel to teach them and seduce them into a sinful lifestyle. Even then, God gave them a chance to repent, but He told them if they did not repent they would be cast out into the great tribulations.

> And unto the angel of the church in Thyatira write; These things saith the Son of God, who hath his eyes like unto a flame of fire, and his feet are like fine brass; I know thy works, and charity, and service, and faith, and thy patience and thy works; and the last to be more than the first. Notwithstanding, I have a few things against thee, because thou sufferest that woman Jezebel, which calleth herself a prophetess, to teach and to seduce my servants to commit fornication, and to eat things sacrificed unto idols. And I gave her space to repent of her fornication; and she repented not. Behold, I will cast her into a bed and them that commit adultery with her into great tribulation, except they repent of their deeds. And I will kill her children with death; and all the churches will know that I am he which searcheth the reins and hearts: and I will give unto every one of you according to your works. But unto you I say, and unto the rest in Thyatira, as many as have not this doctrine, and which have not known the depths of Satan, as they speak; I will put upon you none other burden. But that which ye have already hold fast

till I come. And he that overcometh, and keepeth my works unto the end, to him will I give power over the nations: And he shall rule them with a rod of iron; as the vessels of a potter shall they be broken to shivers: even as I received of my Father. And I will give him the morning star. He that hath an ear, let him hear what the Spirit saith unto the churches.

—REVELATION 2:18–29

The fifth Church Age was Sardis; this lasted from A.D. 1200 to A.D. 1750. This church is also still in the "Dark Ages."

And unto the angel of the church in Sardis write; These things saith he that hath the seven Spirits of God, and the seven stars; I know thy works, that thou hast a name that thou livest, and art dead. Be watchful, and strengthen the things which remain, that are ready to die: for I have not found thy works perfect before God. Remember therefore how thou hast received and heard, and hold fast, and repent. If therefore thou shalt not watch, I will come on thee as a thief, and thou shalt not know what hour I will come upon thee. Thou hast a few names even in Sardis which have not defiled their garments; and they shall walk with me in white: for they are worthy. He that overcometh, the same shall be clothed in white raiment; and I will not blot out his name out of the book of life, but I will confess his name before my Father, and before his angels. He that hath an ear, let him hear what the Spirit saith unto the churches.

—REVELATION 3:1–6

God is talking about a dead church. They have a name that they are alive, but instead they are dead. He wants them to know this and to remember how they had heard and received the gospel at the beginning, and to repent. Even so, there were a few names in Sardis who had not defiled their garments of salvation, and they would walk with Him in white. But for those who did not repent, in their lifetime they would have to overcome by giving their lives for their testimony. Then they also would be clothed in white raiment, and their names would not be blotted out of the Book of Life. Also, Jesus Himself would confess their names before His Father and before the angels. This is the Church Age that saw the Protestant Reformation brought about by Martin Luther in Germany (1483–1546). (See Revelation 3:1–5.)

Martin's father urged him to study law in 1505, but two months later Martin suddenly gave that up and turned to a religious life. It happened one evening while he was walking on the road near Erfurt during a rainstorm. A flash of lightning knocked him to the ground, and he was changed that day. He renounced the world and entered a monastery of the Augustinian Eremites at Erfurt. He studied diligently and was ordained a priest in 1507. And in 1510, he visited Rome on business and became greatly upset with the low moral standards of the church in Rome. A few years later, Pope Leo X, in order to raise money for the rebuilding of the church of St. Peters in Rome, offered promises of forgiveness of sins to all who donated money for the rebuilding of the church. Luther protested by nailing to the door of the Wittenburg Church a list of ninety-five propositions, or theses. This list denied the right of the Pope to give forgiveness for sins by indulgences. Great controversy arose, but Luther defended his idea of "justification by faith." He believed that salvation is possible through trust in God's mercy rather than through penances and other works or righteousness. The Pope ordered Luther to appear before the Cardinal and retract all that he had said. Luther refused to do this unless it could be proved to him, from the

Bible, that he was wrong. After this, Luther broke completely with the church at Rome and denied the divine right of the papacy. He said that the Scriptures were the supreme authority. And in 1520, the Pope issued a proclamation, or bull, condemning Luther's teachings. Luther publicly burned the bull at Wittenburg and continued his teachings. In 1521, the Pope issued a Bull of Excommunication against Luther and demanded that he recant. Luther refused and was outlawed. He went into hiding, and with help from a friend, began to translate the New Testament into the German language. In 1525, Luther married a former nun. His marriage emphasized his rejection of monasticism and celibacy for the clergy. The remainder of Luther's life was spent in writing, preaching, and organizing the Reformed Church in Saxony. Luther's translation of the Bible still remains as the Standard German edition to this day. Luther died on February 18, 1546. This was just before the long-deferred thirty-year war to put down his teachings was about to break out over Europe. His body was carried in state to Wittenburg and was attended by throngs of mourners. He was buried in the Castle Church, to whose door he had nailed the ninety-five theses.[35]

Martin Luther was used of God to bring Christianity back to knowledge of the authority of the Holy Bible. He taught us that we must believe that the Bible is to be interpreted literally. In other words, what it says is what it means. Sometimes we tend to forget that fact.

After this comes the sixth Church Age, which began in 1750, the Church Age of Philadelphia. We are now living in the Philadelphian Church Age. Since the Reformation, our history is familiar to all, so we continue with what the Scriptures have to say about this Church Age. One of the first things that we are reminded of is "That He openeth and no man shutteth, and shutteth and no man openeth." This is talking about the door of salvation: while it is open, no man can shut it, and when it is shut, no man can open it. This door has been open since Pentecost; it is still open now, but this church age will see it closed when Jesus comes in the clouds to take His saints home with him. This will happen in this Church Age. And because this church kept His word and did not deny His name, He will keep us from the hour of temptation, or the time of tribulation that is to come upon all who dwell upon the earth:

> And to the angel of the church in Philadelphia write; These things saith he that is holy, he that is true, he that hath the key of David, he that openeth, and no man shutteth; and shutteth, and no man openeth; I know thy works: behold, I have set before thee an open door, and no man can shut it: for thou hast a little strength, and hast kept my word, and hast not denied my name. Behold, I will make them of the synagogue of Satan, which say they are Jews, and are not, but do lie; behold, I will make them to come and worship before thy feet, and to know that I have loved thee. Because thou hast kept the word of my patience, I also will keep thee from the hour of temptation, which shall come upon all the world, to try them that dwell upon the earth. Behold, I come quickly: hold that fast which thou hast, that no man take thy crown.
>
> —REVELATION 3:7–11

We know that the door will be shut during this Church Age for several reasons. First of all, Jesus reminds us that He opened the door and no man could shut it; then He stated that "He shutteth and no man openeth." That is His statement to us that the door is being shut by Him, and no man can open it. We know by studying the other scriptures in the previous chapter of The Door that this happens when the cry is made and all who have the Spirit of God in them are resurrected. Both the godly and ungodly Christians are in that first resurrection.

> Marvel not at this: for the hour is coming, in the which all that are in the graves shall hear his voice, And shall come forth; they that have done good, unto the resurrection of life; and they that have done evil, unto the resurrection of damnation.
>
> —John 5:28–29

Just as the ten virgins knew that the Lord had come, so will all who are resurrected at that time. How else would they come and worship before "thy feet, and know that he loved them"?

> Behold, I will make them of the synagogue of Satan, which say they are Jews, and are not, but do lie; behold, I will make them to come and worship before thy feet, and to know that I have loved thee.
>
> —Revelation 3:9

Then we have God's promise that we will not be here to have to go through the tribulations: to all who dwell upon the earth!

> Because thou hast kept the word of my patience, I also will keep thee from the hour of temptation, which shall come upon all the world, to try them that dwell upon the earth. Behold, I come quickly: hold that fast which thou hast, that no man take thy crown.
>
> —Revelation 3:10–11

All of the saints, whose robes of salvation were clean and white, are now gone in the air with the Lord in the Rapture. That was the sixth church; there is yet a seventh Church Age that we must talk about. This church is the Laodicean Church. And when we read what the Word has to say about the

Laodicean Church, we realize that there is not one good thing that He has to say about it. Why? Because all of the saints are gone in the Rapture; all of the ungodly saints have been resurrected to go through the tribulations. They are the only ones in the Laodicean Church, which means that this is the church that will miss the Rapture.

These are those from all the Church Ages who did not have enough oil, had spots and blemishes on their robes of salvation, failed to repent in their lifetime, and were left behind. To each of the churches and Church Age, He made them a promise: if they would but overcome when tried, He would not blot out their names from the Book of Life. They must give their lives for their testimonies to be overcomers.

When we think about all of those ungodly Christians being resurrected, given new bodies, and cast out into the earth; that sounds like a lot of people—and it is. But God has also taken care of that. Remember, the ratio of those who are taken and those who are left will be half, or fifty percent.

In the parable of the ten virgins, five were taken and five were left. Then in Matthew 24:40–41 it states: "Then shall two be in the field; the one shall be taken, and the other left. Two women shall be grinding at the mill; the one shall be taken, and the other left." The Lord wanted us to know that He had everything planned, that we would not have anything to worry about. God will take care of the vacuum left by the saints who are caught up with Him in the clouds. There will be an equal number of those who are resurrected to take their place here on earth. And here again is another promise to those who must overcome:

> To him that overcometh will I grant to sit with me in my throne, even as I also overcame, and am set down with my Father in his throne.
>
> —Revelation 3:21

We are being reminded that they must overcome, even as He overcame; that is, by giving their life, just as He did. We are getting ahead of ourselves. Let us go back and see what the scriptures say about the Laodicean Church:

> And unto the angel of the church of the Laodiceans write; These things saith the Amen, the faithful and true witness, the beginning of the creation of God; I know thy works, that thou art neither cold nor hot: I would thou wert cold or hot. So then because thou art lukewarm, and neither cold nor hot, I will spue thee out of my mouth. Because thou sayest, I am rich, and increased with goods, and have need of nothing; and knowest not that thou art wretched, and miserable, and poor, and blind, and naked: I council thee to buy of me gold tried in the fire, that thou mayest be rich; and white raiment, that thou mayest be clothed, and that the shame of thy nakedness do not appear; and annoint thine eyes with eyesalve, that thou mayest see. As many as I love, I rebuke and chasten: be zealous therefore, and repent.
>
> —REVELATION 3:14–19

The Rapture has occurred, with only the lukewarm Christians left. They will be spewed out of His mouth and onto the earth to be tried and tested. They will think that they have it all and will not know that they are wretched, miserable, poor, blind, and naked. He begs them ("I counsel thee") to be willing to be tried in the fire and be made rich in Him. Also, He wants them to be clothed with white raiment, so that they will not be ashamed. And He also begs them to ask Him to open their eyes, so that they may see and understand all that is coming upon them. Even so, He wants them to know that, as many as He loves, He rebukes and chastens; therefore, accept it graciously and repent.

These are all of the ungodly Christians from all of the Church Ages who have been waiting for the first resurrection, to hear the cry and come forth, to meet the Lord in the air. They are and have been (since death, if death has come to them) in heaven, or the kingdom of God, waiting for this glorious event. They don't realize that if their robes of salvation are not white and clean, they will, at that time, be cast out onto the earth. Let us read again those verses in Luke that remind us of this:

> Strive to enter in at the strait gate: for many, I say unto you, will seek to enter in, and shall not be able. When once the master of the house is risen up, and hath shut to the door, and ye begin to stand without, and to knock at the door, saying Lord, Lord, open unto us; and he shall answer and say unto you, I know you not whence ye are: Then shall ye begin to say, We have eaten and drunk in thy presence, and thou hast taught in our streets. But he shall say, I tell you, I know you not whence ye are; depart from me, all ye workers of iniquity. There shall be weeping and gnashing of teeth, when ye shall see Abraham, and Isaac, and Jacob, and all the prophets, in the kingdom of God, and you yourselves thrust out.
>
> —LUKE 13:24–28

This confirms all that we have been saying. God will have only those whose robes are white and clean in His kingdom. He loves those whose robes are white and clean in His kingdom. He loves every one of us, and would that none should perish. But the choice belongs to each of us. We must not only be born again of the Spirit, but we must walk that road here on earth. It is a road that is straight and narrow, a road that leads to our eternal home with Him. Every reference in the Gospels that refer to the weeping and gnashing of teeth are in reference to those who will have missed the Rapture.

How would you feel? Wouldn't you be weeping and gnashing your teeth if you realized that you had missed the Rapture? To have been in the kingdom of God, with all the old prophets, as well as your loved ones and friends who had gone on also, and then to be cast out onto the earth? At that time, you would know that you must go through the tribulations to wash your robe of salvation white. That is a sobering thought. We are reminded again that the door has been closed:

> Behold, I stand at the door and knock: if any man hear my voice, and open the door, I will come in to him, and will sup with him, and he with me.
>
> —REVELATION 3:20

The door of salvation was shut at the time of the Rapture. But those who are behind this door already have salvation and the Spirit of God in them. Now they must wash their robes of salvation so that they are white and clean. Now it is up to each of them to choose to fellowship with the Lord, to open up to Him and allow Him to fellowship with them. This is the choice that each of them who dwell upon the earth must make.

They will need to fellowship with the Lord to be able to overcome all the temptations and trials that will come upon them. There are those who have said, pertaining to Revelation 3:20, that anyone at that time can still be saved. But that is taken out of context. The resurrection and Rapture have occurred, and the door has been shut. The ungodly Christians who have spots or wrinkles in their robe of salvation will be left here on earth; behind that door. And, along with them will be the whole house of Israel, whom God will have resurrected and put His Spirit into them. These, are all destined to go into the time of tribulations. This will come to all who are dwelling on the earth at that time.

And God's Word tells us that of all those who are on the earth during the time of tribulations, only one-third of them will overcome and be victorious:

> And it shall come to pass, that in all the land, saith the LORD, two parts therein shall be cut off and die; but the third shall be left therein. And I will bring the third part through the fire, and will refine them as silver is refined, and will try them as gold is tried: they shall call on my name, and I will hear them: I will say, It is my people: and they shall say, The LORD is my God.
>
> —ZECHARIAH 13:8–9

All of them will have a second chance to have eternal life with our Lord and Savior, Jesus Christ. God's will is that none should perish, but the decision will be up to each of them. They must choose to fellowship with our Lord. God wants only children who love Him and have been tried and tested, and who have proved that love for Him.

For you, that can pertain to the present, while you are alive, or later, if you have your robe of salvation. The alternative is to spend eternity in hell with Satan and his followers. There is no in between. There is life after death. Where will you spend eternity?

Will you be ready to meet the Lord in the air when He comes for us to take us with Him? Or will you be one of those who will be weeping and gnashing your teeth, because you have been left here on earth? And if so, you will be one who is named in the Laodicean Church, the church that will miss the Rapture.

# Chapter 9

# GOD'S CHOSEN PEOPLE

GOD'S CHOSEN PEOPLE are the Jews. Even though they rejected Him, He refused to abandon them. He blinded their eyes, until the fullness of the Gentiles comes in. (See Romans 11:25.) He then turned to the Gentiles to get a bride. But He has an everlasting covenant with the Jews. Romans, chapter 11 gives all the details of His relationship with the Jews. He promises to take away their sins:

> For I would not, brethren, that ye should be ignorant of this mystery, lest ye should be wise in your own conceits; that blindness in part is happened to Israel, until the fulness of the Gentiles be come in. And so all Israel shall be saved: as it is written, There shall come out of Sion the Deliverer, and shall turn away ungodliness from Jacob: For this is my covenant unto them, when I shall take away their sins.
>
> —ROMANS 11:25–27

All through the Bible, within the Old and New Testaments, God has made this promise to them. He wants the whole house of Israel to be saved. He will raise them up, in the first resurrection, put His Spirit in them, place them in their own land, and send 144,000 Jews to preach and minister to them. That is how much He loves the Jews, the whole house of Israel. Even into the millennial reign, children will be born to them, and their numbers will multiply.

> That when the LORD thy God will turn thy captivity, and have compassion upon thee, and will return and gather thee from all the nations, whither the LORD thy God hath scattered thee. If any of thine be driven out unto the outmost parts of heaven, from thence will the LORD thy God gather thee, and from thence will he fetch thee: And the LORD thy God will bring thee into the land which thy fathers possessed, and thou shalt possess it; and he will do thee good, and multiply thee above thy fathers.
> —DEUTERONOMY 30:3–5

The whole house of Israel will be resurrected and gathered from all nations and all parts of heaven in the first resurrection. God will put His Spirit into them and lead them back to their fathers' land. Their eyes will no longer be blinded to the gospel, for the fullness of the Gentiles will come in. The Rapture has occurred for the bride of Christ. Now the Jews must hear the gospel—and God knows that it must be Jews He sends to them with the gospel so that they will listen and receive. And that will be the 144,000 from all the twelve tribes of Israel:

> And I saw another angel ascending from the east, having the seal of the living God: and he cried with a loud voice to the four angels, to whom it was given to hurt the

earth and the sea, Saying, Hurt not the earth, neither the sea, nor the trees, till we have sealed the servants of our God in their foreheads. And I heard the number of them which were sealed: and there were sealed a hundred and forty and four thousand of all the tribes of the children of Israel. Of the tribe of Juda were sealed twelve thousand. Of the tribe of Reuben were sealed twelve thousand. Of the tribe of Gad were sealed twelve thousand. Of the tribe of Aser were sealed twelve thousand. Of the tribe of Nephthalim were sealed twelve thousand. Of the tribe of Manasses were sealed twelve thousand. Of the tribe of Simeon were sealed twelve thousand. Of the tribe of Levi were sealed twelve thousand. Of the tribe of Issachar were sealed twelve thousand. Of the tribe of Zabulon were sealed twelve thousand. Of the tribe of Joseph were sealed twelve thousand. Of the tribe of Benjamin were sealed twelve thousand.

—REVELATION 7:2–8

Now that we know who they are, let us see where they came from and how. First of all, we know that God would send only the best to minister to His chosen people. I believe that these were great men of old, prophets, more than likely, who walked the earth long ago and taught and preached. There are possibly even the prophets that God used to pen the words that are on the pages of our precious Bible.

God's Word tells us that they, having been the first fruits unto God, will be pure and without fault before the Lord. They were resurrected at Christ's coming, given new bodies, and made alive as "first fruits." Let us see what the Scriptures say about that:

But now is Christ risen from the dead, and become the first fruits of them that slept. For since by man came death, by man came also the resurrection of the dead. For as in Adam all die, even so in Christ shall all be made alive. But every man in his order: Christ the first fruits; afterward they that are Christ's at his coming.

—1 CORINTHIANS 15:20–23

By these words we know that they are among the first fruits of God, being resurrected at Christ's coming, in the first resurrection. They are the chosen of God from among men, sealed with God's seal in their foreheads, given new bodies and made alive here on earth, and commissioned by God to go and preach to the house of Israel and bring them to a saving knowledge of the gospel. Again, this is for all who will receive the gospel. Revelation also tells us who they were:

These are they which were not defiled with women; for they are virgins. These are they which follow the Lamb whithersoever he goeth. These were redeemed from among men, being the first fruits unto God and to the Lamb. And in their mouth was found no guile: for they are without fault before the throne of God.

—REVELATION 14:4–5

These verses tell us that the 144,000 had been in the kingdom of God, awaiting the first resurrection day. They followed the Lamb, which is our Lord, Jesus Christ, wherever He went. And because they were in the kingdom of God, they were virgins. Remember the parable of the ten virgins in Matthew 25. Being in the kingdom of God made them virgins before the Lord. The hundred and forty-four thousand will be without fault before the throne of God. Man, being of Adam, shall all die. But, because we are Christ's, at His coming, we shall all be made alive. First comes death, then the resurrection: Christ, the first fruits, then all who belong to Christ when He comes.

So you see, these 144,000 will be among the first fruits unto God. They will be chosen and redeemed from among men. They will be resurrected at Christ's coming and sealed in their foreheads. Then they will be sent back to their homeland, to the house of Israel. There they will preach to the Jews and bring them to a saving knowledge of the gospel. Now let us go back and read the first three verses of the fourteenth chapter of Revelation.

Here, they have completed their work on earth and are with the Lamb. And as they stand before the throne and the elders and the four beasts, they sing a new song, one that no one else could sing. They will have done something that no others have ever done before, therefore, no others could ever sing their song:

> And I looked, and lo, a Lamb stood on the mount Sion, and with him a hundred forty and four thousand, having his Father's name written in their foreheads. And I heard a voice from heaven; as the voice of many waters, and as the voice of a great thunder: and I heard the voice of harpers harping with their harps: And they sung as it were a new song before the throne, and before the four beasts, and the elders: and no man could learn that song but the hundred and forty and four thousand, which were redeemed from the earth.
> —REVELATION 14:1–3

That, indeed, will be a song to sing, a story to tell: they had lived for the Lord in their lifetime, died, and went into the kingdom of God; will be resurrected in the first resurrection, and changed, given new bodies; brought back to earth, sealed with the Father's name in their foreheads, so that nothing here on earth could harm them; (they will be here during the tribulation period); and able to preach to the whole house of Israel, who had also been resurrected, and God's Spirit put in them, and given another chance, to be tried and tested, and overcome; and then the 144,000 ascended back to heaven and will be before the throne, singing a song only they can sing. Isaiah, the prophet foretold this in 712 B.C.:

> He will swallow up death in victory; and the Lord God will wipe away tears from off all faces; and the rebuke of his people shall he take away from off all the earth: for the Lord hath spoken it. And it shall be said in that day, Lo, this is our God; we have waited for him, and he will save us: this is the Lord; we have waited for him, we will be glad and rejoice in his salvation.
>
> —Isaiah 25:8–9

Their eyes will be opened; they will be able to see that He is Lord and has come to save them, and they will rejoice in His salvation. The Jews are and were God's chosen people. Pray for the Jews.

Death is swallowed up in victory at the first resurrection. All who go into the tribulations from the first resurrection will not be hurt by the second death. The second death will be when they must give their lives for their testimony.

> Blessed and holy is he that hath part in the first resurrection: on such the second death hath no power, but they shall be priests of God and of Christ, and shall reign with him a thousand years.
>
> —Revelation 20:6

Death has truly been swallowed up in victory at that time. There will be no fear of the second death for all who are Christ's. They will give their lives willingly for their testimony:

And I saw thrones, and they sat upon them, and judgment was given unto them: and I saw the souls of them that were beheaded for the witness of Jesus, and for the Words of God, and which had not worshipped the beast, neither his image, neither had received his mark upon their foreheads, or in their hands; and they lived and reigned with Christ a thousand years.

—REVELATION 20:4

Paul's letter to the Romans in the eleventh chapter talks about the Jews:

For if the casting away of them be the reconciling of the world, what shall the receiving of them be, but life from the dead?

—ROMANS 11:15

For God hath concluded them all in unbelief, that he might have mercy upon all.

—ROMANS 11:32

For I would not, brethren, that ye should be ignorant of this mystery, lest ye should be wise in your own conceits; that blindness in part is happened to Israel, until the fullness of the Gentiles be come in. And so all Israel shall be saved: as it is written, There shall come out of Sion the Deliverer, and shall turn away ungodliness from Jacob: For this is my covenant unto them, when I shall take away their sins.

—ROMANS 11:25–27

Seventy weeks are allotted by God upon His chosen people and the holy city of Jerusalem. Sixty-nine weeks are history; the seventieth week will come after the fullness of the Gentiles comes in—when He comes for His bride in the first resurrection, and

111

the Rapture of the saints who are ready and have gone on and met the Lord in the air, to be raptured and taken with Him. The whole house of Israel will be resurrected with God's Spirit put in them. They will then face the seventieth week, which is seven years, to make reconciliation for their iniquity, accept the Lord as their Savior, and have victory over death and the grave.

> Seventy weeks are determined upon thy people and upon thy holy city, to finish the transgression, and to make an end of sins, and to make reconciliation for iniquity, and to bring in everlasting righteousness, and to seal up the vision and prophecy, and to anoint the most Holy.
>
> —Daniel 9:24

And again, God's promise to the whole house of Israel that they will be saved, that they are His chosen people:

> The hand of the LORD was upon me, and carried me out in the spirit of the LORD, and set me down in the midst of the valley which was full of bones, And caused me to pass by them round about: and, behold, there were very many in the open valley; and, lo, they were very dry. And he said unto me, Son of man, can these bones live? And I answered, O Lord God, thou knowest. Again he said unto me, Prophesy upon these bones, and say unto them, O ye dry bones, hear the word of the LORD. Thus saith the Lord God unto these bones; Behold, I will cause breath to enter into you, and ye shall live: And I will lay sinews upon you, and will bring up flesh upon you, and cover you with skin, and put breath in you, and ye shall live; and ye shall know that I am the LORD. So I prophesied as I was commanded: and as I prophesied, there was a noise, and behold a shaking, and the bones came together, bone to his bone. And when I beheld, lo, the sinews and the flesh came up upon them, and

the skin covered them above: but there was no breath in them. Then he said unto me, Prophesy unto the wind, prophesy, son of man, and say to the wind, Thus saith the Lord God; Come from the four winds, O breath, and breathe upon these slain, that they may live. So I prophesied as he commanded me, and the breath came into them, and they lived, and stood upon their feet, an exceeding great army. Then he said unto me, Son of man, these bones are the whole house of Israel: behold, they say, Our bones are dried, and our hope is lost: we are cut off for our parts. Therefore prophesy and say unto them, Thus saith the Lord God; Behold, O my people, I will open your graves, and cause you to come up out of your graves, and bring you into the land of Israel. And ye shall know that I am the LORD, when I have opened your graves, O my people, and brought you up out of your graves, And shall put my spirit in you, and ye shall live, and I shall place you in your own land: then shall ye know that I the LORD have spoken it, and performed it, saith the LORD.

—EZEKIEL 37:1–14

The whole house of Israel, as a whole, have died without the Spirit of God in them. Because of disobedience, God had blinded their eyes and closed their ears to the gospel. Therefore, when they died, they did not have the Spirit of God in them. That is why it is said in Ezekiel 37:11, "Our hope is lost, we are cut off for our parts." And God's words through Ezekiel the prophet were, "When I have opened your graves, and brought you up out of your graves, and shall put my Spirit in you, and ye shall live, and I shall place you in your own land" (Ezek. 37:13).

This tells us that God will resurrect them first from the grave, and then He will put his Spirit in them, and they shall live. They are truly God's chosen people. No others in the Bible will have that privilege.

As Gentiles, we must have God's Spirit in us when we die, or we will not hear the cry when it is made to come forth. We must have believed, repented, and received Him as Lord of our life to be able to hear His voice when He calls for us. These are Jesus' own words from John's gospel:

> My sheep hear my voice, and I know them, and they follow me: And I give them eternal life; and they shall never perish, neither shall any man pluck them out of my hand.
>
> —JOHN 10:27–28

Those who do not hear will be the sinners who have died without ever receiving Him as Lord of their lives, or blasphemers.

The fullness of the Gentiles will have come in, at this time, and the time for the Jews will have begun. Their seventieth week will begin so that they might be brought into the kingdom of God. All of the house of Israel will have their second chance, just as God promised them that they would. God was angry with His chosen people, but they were still His chosen ones, and He had made a covenant with them. His covenants cannot be broken:

> For my name's sake will I defer mine anger, and for my praise will I refrain for thee, that I cut thee not off. Behold, I have refined thee, but not with silver; I have chosen thee in the furnace of affliction. For mine own sake, even for mine own sake, will I do it: for how should my name be polluted? and I will not give my glory unto another. Hearken unto me, O Jacob and Israel, my called; I am he; I am the first, I also am the last. Mine hand also hath laid the foundation of the earth, and my right hand

hath spanned the heavens: when I call unto them, they
stand up together.

—Isaiah 48:9–13

They must go through the furnace of affliction, which is
the tribulations that are to come upon the earth; the seventieth week promised to his own people. But through it all, God
will be with them. He will dry up waters, that they might pass
through on dry land; just as it was for Israel, when they came
out of the land of Egypt:

> And it shall come to pass in that day, that the Lord shall
> set his hand again the second time to recover the rem-
> nant of his people, which shall be left, from Assyria, and
> from Egypt, and from Pathros, and from Cush, and from
> Elam, and from Shinar, and from Hamath, and from the
> islands of the sea. And he shall set up an ensign for the
> nations, and shall assemble the outcasts of Israel, and
> gather together the dispersed of Judah from the four
> corners of the earth. And the Lord shall utterly destroy
> the tongue of the Egyptian sea; and with his mighty wind
> shall he shake his hand over the river, and shall smite it in
> the seven streams, and make men go over dryshod. And
> there shall be an highway for the remnant of his people,
> which shall be left, from Assyria; like as it was to Israel in
> the day that he came up out of the land of Egypt.
>
> —Isaiah 11:11–12, 15–16

Is not that just like the Lord? Over the years there have been
many skeptics discussing and even denying the fact that God
could part the waters of the sea for His people to go through
on dry ground. And here we see that He is going to do it again.
This is in the future, near future, during the time of tribulation
here on earth. He is going to bring His chosen people from

115

the four corners of the earth and into their own land. God will do all that is necessary to bring them back, including parting the waters for them. The reporters and the television crews will have a field day. Pictures don't lie; what will the skeptics say then? I am sure the good Lord will get a laugh out of that scene. In the next chapter, God's people are praising Him for what He has done for them:

> And in that day thou shalt say, O LORD, I will praise thee: though thou wast angry with me, thine anger is turned away, and thou comfortedst me. Behold, God is my salvation; I will trust, and not be afraid: for the LORD JEHOVAH is my strength and my song; he also is become my salvation. Therefore with joy shall ye draw water out of the wells of salvation. And in that day shall ye say, Praise the LORD, call upon his name, declare his doings among the people, make mention that his name is exalted. Sing unto the LORD; for he hath done excellent things; this is known in all the earth. Cry and shout, thou inhabitant of Zion: for great is the Holy One of Israel in the midst of thee.
>
> —ISAIAH 12:1–6

Would not your joy be overflowing if you were with them at that time? They will have died without hope and in despair. Many of them will have gone to other countries. But God will bring them up out of their graves, put His Spirit in them, give them new bodies. He will put life and breath in them and then help them to return to the homeland of their fathers. That is when He will part the waters of the river for them to be able to go through on dry ground to return to their homeland. God will have only a people who have been tried, as in the fire, either in their lifetime or during the tribulations, and have overcome. He will accept nothing less from each of us, Jews and Gentiles. They will know that Jesus Christ is Lord!

# NOTES

**Chapter 8**
**The Church That Will Miss the Rapture**

1. Henry H. Halley, *Halley's Bible Handbook*, 24th Edition (Grand Rapids: Zondervan Publishing House, 1965), 685.

2. Ibid., 683.

3. Ibid., 684.

4. Ibid., 684.

5. Ibid., 632.

6. Ibid., 635.

7. Ibid., 636.

8. Ibid., 640.

9. Ibid., 637.

10. Ibid., 701.

11. Philip Schaff, *History of the Christian Church*, Vol. II, 5th Edition (Grand Rapids, Wm. B. Eerdmans Publishing Co., 1910), 66.

12. Ibid., 68.

13. Ibid., 69.

14. Ibid., 69.

15. Halley, 704.

16. Schaff, 72.

17. Ibid., 66.

18. Ibid., 68.

19. Ibid., 69.

20. Ibid., 71.

21. Ibid., 72.

22. Leon L. Bram, editor, *Funk & Wagnall's New Encyclopedia*, Vol. 6. (INFO), 448.

23. Eusebius, *The History of the Church From Christ to*

*Constantine* (Dorset Press, 1984), 402.

    24. Halley, 759.

    25. Ibid., 760.

    26. Ibid., 761.

    27. Ibid.

    28. Schaff, 464.

    29. Halley, 774.

    30. Ibid., 775.

    31. Ibid., 776.

    32. Ibid., 776.

    33. Ibid., 768.

    34. Ibid., 776.

    35. *Compton's Pictured Encyclopedia* (Chicago, IL: F.E. Compton Co., 1965).

## To Contact the Author

Colene Ledford
P.O. Box 2722
Apopka, FL  32704-2722

**Web site:** http://hometown.aol.com/cledford4711/